Always Be
AMAZING!

Jim Hunt

"Almost 20 years ago, when I first became a newly-elected local official, I made it a priority to seek out inspiring leaders who could help me better understand this complex and critical new role. I had the good fortune of having a mentor in Jim Hunt, a wise and seasoned leader who readily shared his insights into the world of local politics. We both came from similar small cities at the time. It was from watching and listening to him that I learned the inherent qualities of a true leader, and of the courage that it takes to stand up to one's convictions. With Jim's encouragement, I stepped out of my comfort zone and worked at becoming the kind of leader I aspired to be. From a city council member and subsequently a Mayor, to the first female Latina president of the National League of Cities, I always sought out Jim's counsel and advice with regard to making the lives of people in cities more meaningful.

I find I am still watching, and learning from Jim. His books inspire us all to find our own unique role in shaping our communities."

Marie Lopez Rogers
Former Mayor, Avondale AZ &
Past President of the National League of Cities

"Jim Hunt has spent a lifetime watching and learning what makes cities successful. He has a remarkable ability to glean the best characteristics of every city he visits. His writings reveal a man who is keenly perceptive and has a deep love for our communities"

Ted Ellis
Mayor, Bluffton, Indiana
Past President, National League of Cities

"Jim and I have worked together as national leaders in government. Committing himself to understanding and listening about what makes cities great is his passion. You will feel it in his writing - and you will be empowered."

Valerie Brown
Past President
National Association of Counties

"In *Amazing Cities,* Jim Hunt has reduced the formula for a successful city to just a few basic elements: positive thinking, creative planning and attention to detail on the part of leaders and empowerment of its citizens. Hunt reminds us that people, especially young people, want to live in places that are inclusive and environmentally sustainable. His examples of successful cities inspire us to seek to make our communities.... *Amazing!*"

Lee Beaulac
President, Beaulac Associates, LLC
Board Member Emeritus, NCRC

"Jim Hunt has written the KISS (Keep It Simple Stupid) primer for local governments. With his vast local, national and international experience, he gives us 7 basic action items for successful cities. As a former mayor who has worked closely with Jim, here's my advice to local government officials.... buy this book and follow these steps, you won't regret it!"

Bill Byrne
Former Mayor, City of Morgantown,
West Virginia

"Jim Hunt is a leading edge thinker with a plethora of practical and actionable advice he shares in this book on how to make cities Amazing. His personal experiences with leaders and historical events provide vivid images of actions the reader can take from the book."

Frank Jenio, Ph.D.
President, Center for
Thinking & Collaboration LLC

"Jim Hunt's college basketball years were long ago, but he can still take it to the hoop when it matters. In *The Amazing City* he chronicles great work by many leaders, managers and citizens to make our cities, towns and neighborhoods more vibrant and attractive. He dispenses effective prescriptions based on his first-hand experience and amazing ability to listen to people who know what they are doing. It matters."

Ellis Hankins
Visiting Professor at UNC-Chapel Hill,
NC State and Duke University
and Retired Executive Director,
NC League of Municipalities

"Amazing cities are only possible if amazing people work to make them happen - over my 14 years as a local elected official, Jim Hunt epitomized what an amazing leader should be! His humble, compassionate and inquisitive spirit showed us the way, and his book will continue his teachings into the next generation of city officials."

Bev Perry
Former Mayor
Brea, CA

"This book is not only a roadmap to create amazing cities, but a roadmap as to how we should live life."

Colleen Landkamer
Past President of the National
Association of Counties
2000 County Leader of the Year by
American City and County Magazine

"There is no shortage of theories about the secret sauce for city success. James Hunt's focus on the attitude of cities sets him apart from many experts who focus only on place-making, talent and innovation. A successful city must have all of these elements, but a city must have something more or it will not succeed. It must believe in itself. James Hunt understands this, and reading his great book will get us closer to creating truly amazing cities."

Lee Fisher
President and CEO
CEO's for Cities

"Jim Hunt is 'Amazing'! He has traveled to more cities - large and small, in the US as well as around the world – than most people get to in many lifetimes. But what really impresses me is that he has learned something important of general applicability from each of the places he's visited. If you're feeling depressed by the inertia, infighting, and ineffectiveness at the national level of government, this book is for you – new ideas and stories of success at the local level fly from the pages in every chapter. I feel better about the future just hearing Jim's insights."

Paul Helmke
Indiana University Professor
and Director of Civic Leaders Center
Past-President of U. S. Conference of Mayors

"Jim Hunt has traveled the world visiting and working with cities large and small. The result of those experiences can be found in his book *The Amazing City*. This insightful publication is a seven step guide for all those who strive to build their community into an amazing place."

Doug Echols
Mayor, Rock Hill, SC

This book offers motivating, innovating, and stimulating steps that inspire a solid foundation to achieve successes creating an Amazing City anywhere in the world! Thanks Jim Hunt, an Amazing Leader who loves All Cities!!!

Vince Williams
Mayor, Union City, Georgia

"Jim Hunt has set the stage in his "Amazing Cities..." that mayors have modeled far and wide. Amazing cities are epicenters of positive connectivity. It's a place where family, work, friends, faith and wellness all form a safety web of inclusiveness. A must read for leaders and policy makers."

Krisanna Clark
Mayor, Sherwood, Oregon

"Jim Hunt knows that creating an Amazing City takes compassion, commitment and hard work. His actions and innovations have helped influence the Not In Our Town movement to stop hate and intolerance across the country. We look forward to sharing his lessons with our network."

Patrice O'Neill,
Founder and Executive Producer
Not In Our Town/The Working Group

"Local leaders in cities and towns across Alabama, like those across America, face an ever-changing landscape. From advances in technology to global competition to managing regionalism, all while juggling the every-day issues facing them, *The Amazing City* helps the reader prioritize and innovate—a must for the successful leader! The seven principles in *The Amazing City* are game changers for local leaders across our nation to improve the lives of the citizens they serve."

Jim Byard, Jr.,
Director, Alabama Department of
Economic and Community Affairs

"Much of American history suggests that commitment to racial justice and inclusiveness, if it is ever to be found within government, must be found in national government. We are accustomed to the scenario where national policy is shaped by fundamental values such as equality, and where state and local government have been compelled, to one degree or another, to follow suit. Jim Hunt's life work is the compelling evidence that this is not the way it has to be; that local government can be the context for creative approaches to these challenges, and that truly good local leadership can build communities where we can all be our best selves."

Paul R. Sheridan,
West Virginia Lawyer and Activist
Former Head of the West Virginia
Attorney General's Civil Rights Division

"Demographic realities increasingly dictate the importance of cities as the preferred habitat for more and more Americans. And it is critical that those cities evolve to not only handle the basic needs of the rising number of residents but that they also respond comprehensively to the quality of needs inherent in this reemergence of cities as the preferred community.

People are not just looking for the conveniences of cities (transportation and nearby services) but rather they are seeking a more holistic lifestyle, indeed an "Amazing City", as Jim Hunt has accurately paraphrased it.

People want a safe, vibrant, clean, dynamic and livable city in which to live, one where the quality of life is central to those communities. Such cities evolve intentionally, not accidentally. Community leaders will find important bright lines in Jim Hunt's seminal work on the considerations and elements needed to build these Amazing Cities, a must read."

John Taylor,
President and CEO
National Community Reinvestment Coalition

"Jim Hunt draws on his extensive experience as a highly effective local government leader to create an engaging and practical handbook for elected officials and policymakers as well as business and community leaders who want to build healthy, inclusive cities in our rapidly changing world."

Rob Corcoran,
founder of Hope in the Cities,
and author of Trustbuilding: An Honest Conversation
on Race, Reconciliation and Responsibility

THE AMAZING CITY

7 Steps to Creating an Amazing City

JAMES C. HUNT

THE ELIM
GROUP

ISBN 978-0-9855660-1-2

*Dedicated to my father, Rex B. Hunt
and Pastor David D.A. Kates.*

*You gave me a passion
for local government and
the power of ordinary people
doing extraordinary things.*

CONTENTS

Acknowledgements

I can remember standing in the White House next to the painting of President John F. Kennedy, awaiting a meeting with President Obama and thinking about my strange and exciting journey from a small town in West Virginia to leading the National League of Cities, the nation's oldest and largest organization representing America's cities. As the old farmer told his son, after finding a turtle atop a fence post, "You can be sure that he didn't get there by himself!" This book has been written with the help and guidance of thousands of wonderful people who have been a part of my life, some for a lifetime and some for a shorter duration.

I am forever bonded to a loyal cadre of friends that have made me a better person. My childhood friend, Ron Fragale, has been with me through thick and thin and we have never forgotten our beginnings in the Montpelier neighborhood on the "wrong side of the tracks" in Clarksburg.

The citizens of Clarksburg, West Virginia gave me the opportunity to represent them for over a quarter of a century and in doing so, gave me a laboratory in which to research the formulas for creating an Amazing City. During my tenure, I was able to see the incredible work of dedicated professionals who loved their city and spent their careers making it better. I served with dozens of councilmembers and though we didn't always agree, I count them as some of my closest friends. The City Managers and City Clerks that I had the opportunity to work with hold a special place in my heart for the difficult work that they do in a political environment on

1

public display at all hours.

Mayors Tom Flynn and Pastor David D.A. Kates are special people to me and brought dignity to city government in ways that I am forever indebted. When Pastor Kates became the first African-American Mayor in the history of our city, I knew that nothing I could ever accomplish could eclipse that day for my pride in our city. Annette Wright, our City Clerk has also served as my model when people would ask me to describe the person who was the heart of our city. I'd like to note each of the special people in the city but I fear that the book would grow too heavy to carry.

The West Virginia Municipal League played a critical role in my development as a public official and Lisa Dooley, the Executive Director has been a friend and supporter every step of my journey. Learning from the staff and members of the League has given me many of the lessons outlined in the book and I cannot thank them enough for their friendship over the years. So many wonderful people have passed through the League and I miss those who are no longer with us but will never forget their contributions and friendships. The League is an incredible leadership development organization and I am so impressed as new leaders continually refresh the pool of talent and continue a distinguished legacy.

The National League of Cities gave me the opportunity to develop as a leader and gain thousands of new friends and colleagues. Meeting elected officials from throughout the United States gave me a perspective that few are able to receive. The diversity and inclusive nature of the organization centered my life as a public official and made me a better person. Former Executive Director Don Borut and current Executive Director

Clarence Anthony have been outstanding leaders and provided me with opportunities for which I will be forever grateful. The staff have been some of my closest friends and I am so very grateful for their dedication to America's cities. My NLC family is truly a family. We know each other's families and we celebrate each other's successes and mourn each other's losses.

As part of my participation in the National League of Cities, it opened the door for travel to the United Cities and Local Governments (UCLG) meetings throughout the world. Hours of meetings and hard work gave way to seeing sights that I could only dream about as a young man. They say you don't know someone well until you travel with them and I gained lifelong friendships on many international trips. I will always be grateful to Don Borut for giving me the opportunity to represent the National League of Cities and lead delegations in a quest for better relations with cities throughout the world. Ted and Marge Ellis, Don and Carol Borut, Clarence Anthony, Jim Brooks and others made my wife Pam and I feel like international celebrities as we trekked the globe.

When I embarked on a career as a speaker and writer, I gained a whole new set of incredible friends and colleagues. My friend and fellow author, Mike Conduff has given me the confidence to write and share my thoughts and ideas. Brian Davis, a superstar salesman, has been a great friend as we travel the country on behalf of clients. Mike and Brian asked me many years ago if I wanted to have a lot of fun and possibly make some money and I have not looked back. My other colleague, Dr. Frank Jenio of The Reinvent Project has also encouraged me to keep "reinventing" myself and helping others. My friends at the Pittsburgh Chapter of the National Speaker's Association are a steady force in my life. I cannot measure how much I have grown as a professional speaker and person from advice gained at the NSA meetings.

While I may never be confused with a famous writer, my skills have been made immeasurably better by my friendship with a tremendous editor, Leigh Merrifield. Leigh has been a faithful colleague during my tenure as a columnist for the Harrison County News & Journal and has polished up my submissions into a somewhat readable experience. Writing a weekly column is one of the best ways to find your voice and get into the habit of putting your thoughts on paper.

My final acknowledgements are for my wonderful family. My wife Pam has allowed me to pursue my dreams while she has maintained our beautiful home and made sure I remembered the important things in life. My children, Sarah and her husband Matt and Jason and his girlfriend Staci have grown into fantastic adults who have picked up the mantle of service. My grandchildren, Ali, Avery and Emery give me a passion to write, knowing that they will live in the world we leave them. I have been blessed to still have my mother in my life along with my brother Tom and sisters, Dianne and Mary.

I could not close this without mention of my dog, Jack. He has been a faithful companion and kept me company on the many hours that I have spent writing this book. They say in politics that if you need a friend, get a dog! I could not agree more and have found a good one in Jack.

Publisher's Note

My first National League of Cities Conference was in 1979, and sometime in the 1980's I started seeing the same tall West Virginian at all the meetings. For the next twenty years we had what I call a "conference acquaintance." As long as Jim Hunt had on his badge (with increasing numbers of ribbons) and I had on mine we could call each other by our first names, but otherwise we just waved or nodded or talked about the weather at the meetings. We traveled in different circles, mine on the administrative track and his on the elected, so it was in the hallways or registration lines we most often spoke.

That changed in 2006 when I, now in my post local government career, was hired to do a Good Governance keynote speech for the North Dakota Municipal League Annual Conference in Minot. Connie Sprynczynatyk, the then Executive Director of NDML also invited Jim, as the NLC President-Elect, to participate. As the result of having several days to spend together and seeing each other present we realized we had lots of alignment in philosophy on how to help cities grow stronger and began speaking to conferences and symposia together.

This was especially fun when we did Council/Manager relationship talks and training. Jim would take the Mayor or Council Member (elected official) side, and I would take the City Manager (appointed official) side and we would "interpret" to the audience for each other. While meant to be hyperbole, these exaggerations helped make the point that often times what you hear is indeed dependent on where you sit.

In 2009 we co-authored ***Bottom Line Green – How America's Cities are Saving the Planet (and Money Too!)*** with our friend and colleague Brian Davis, and over the course of the next many years traveled to hundreds of cities across the country, North America and (in Jim's case) world-wide to spread the messages of good governance, sustainability, and leadership. Jim Hunt's genius in each of the communities was that he could seize on something in that town or city that was truly "amazing." And, fortunately for all of us, Jim began capturing these insights for his website and passion, amazingcities.org.

A gifted writer with excellent story telling skills, it is always fun to read Jim's insights on local government. It is also incredibly entertaining to watch him in his element at NLC or in any local government's elected officials' office. His charisma, personal charm and innate ability to communicate put everyone from the receptionist to the Mayor at ease and willing to share their views on what makes their town amazing.

I know that you will have an amazing time reading *The Amazing City*!

Mike Conduff
Denton, TX
2016

Foreword

By Cleveland Councilman Matt Zone
National League of Cities President-2017

Much has been written about the problems and challenges of our American cities, but few authors have the perspective of James C. Hunt, a former president of the National League of Cities, who has served nearly three decades in local government.

In his new book, *The Amazing City — Seven Steps to Creating an Amazing City,* Jim Hunt draws on his experience as a mayor and a legislator in Clarksburg, West Virginia, and his extensive world travels, studying the workings and policy procedures of municipal governments.

As a councilman myself, reading Jim's book gave me an appreciation of how he laid out the challenges public officials face in governing cities, big and small, and how he shows us that at the core of municipal government is "Community" with a capital "C."

You might say Jim and I are on the same page, no pun intended, in our perspectives on how urban communities, some more diverse than others, must be connected internally and beyond their boundaries in terms of economy, revitalization, innovation and social services.

Many books have been written on how to fix cities by people who have never balanced a city budget or worked with neighborhood groups to effect change.

Jim Hunt's parallel career in housing (Manager for WV Housing Development Fund) and community development work (Executive Director of Sunnyside Up-Campus Neighborhoods Revitalization Corporation in Morgantown, WV) has allowed him to see local government from multiple perspectives, as a policy maker, practitioner and community advocate.

There is no shortage of theories about what makes cities amazing. Some experts argue that geography matters more than ever and success depends on physical capital and authentic placemaking. Others say that in a knowledge economy, cities must build human capital and creative talent. Some insist that social capital and economic opportunity ultimately define the soul of a city. Still others predict that the future city is about smart digital capital and harnessing the power of technology.

Each of these theories alone is wrong. A successful city and town must have all of these elements.

Our cities and towns succeed if they are well-connected, both internally and to the wider world, they are fertile places for innovation and entrepreneurship, they nurture, retain, and attract talent, and each city invests in its own distinctive characteristics and strengths. Economic growth and development is about linking and leveraging a city's distinctive assets of people, place, and opportunity.

Cities must be constantly learning, reinventing, sharing and connecting, which, as Jim and I know so well, are components baked into the mission of the National League of Cities, of which I am fortunate to serve as its president in 2017.

The NLC is a network of American cities and towns, drawing on the strengths of urban innovations and offering resources for meeting challenges. It is a valuable resource.

I am encouraged by the passion and commitment of the leaders to address inequities and build more equitable, inclusive communities. NLC is uniquely positioned to provide local elected officials the tools, techniques and resources to prepare them to advance the conversation and translate these important conversations into action.

And like the writings of Jim Hunt, it is a laudatory testimony to Community.

Introduction

"Even though the future seems far away, it is actually beginning right now."
Mattie Stepanek

I'm often asked my opinion on what cities will look like in the future. While I don't profess to be a fortune teller, I think that there are some interesting things happening that might predict a very healthy future for cities. More and more people live in cities and the worldwide trend is a massive shift from rural areas to heavily populated cities. Cities have massive investments in infrastructure that cannot be duplicated in sparsely populated areas. Likewise, schools and other quality of life attractions need populous areas to succeed. Younger people are gravitating to places that don't require a vehicle and the thought of mowing a massive yard is increasingly less attractive to the millennial generation.

The rush to the suburbs was fueled by the automobile in the 50's and many of the less populated suburban areas are now bursting at the seams. The Phoenix area is a good example of this phenomenon with cities like Scottsdale, Mesa, Avondale and others doubling population in just a few years. With retirees, tourists, corporate headquarters and others flocking to Arizona, few people are choosing to be outside of these growing cities. As residents' needs change, they simply move to another close by city instead of heading to the country like their parents and grandparents.

Medical care is also driving the move to the cities. As

Baby Boomers require more and more medical care, few want to be too far from the medical specialists that are treating them. Places like Minneapolis, Cleveland, Baltimore and Boston have attracted new residents that are employed by the medical centers located in their cities. This trend has no sign of slowing down and with more and more innovations in the medical field, many cities may rely solely on a regional medical center and the associated services to sustain their economy.

Recreation is another driver of the move to the cities. Sports teams, water parks and other recreation venues attract millions of people each year and support thousands of jobs. The interesting part of this sector is that cities of all sizes can participate. Large cities do well with professional sports teams but even smaller cities can do great business with minor league sports. On a recent trip to Durham, North Carolina, I learned that the Durham Bulls, minor league baseball team, attracts over half a million fans per year. Minor league hockey, basketball, volleyball and other sports, give cities an increasing amount of opportunities to develop a fan base in all size communities.

Technology is also a big driver in the move to cities. Broadband access and technology support is easier to obtain in cities than in rural areas. Cities are also great customers for new technology and things like LED street lighting and solar panels are gaining a foothold on city streets. Additionally, those young people who are the innovators in the technology economy are dependent on working with others in the field. They need access to each other and cities are the perfect incubators for these growing businesses.

This book is designed to describe the steps that are

necessary to create an Amazing City. The steps are
aspirational and are designed to serve as a blueprint to
lay the plan for what will be a lifelong pursuit. The steps
as described in **Part One** are:

- ATTITUDE
- MOTIVATION
- ATTENTION TO DETAIL
- "ZING"
- INCLUSIVENESS
- NEIGHBORHOOD EMPOWERMENT
- GREEN AWARENESS

Part Two of the book will give examples of innovative ideas that are taking place in cities throughout the
world and can serve as a stimulus to discussion and
a starting point to begin developing strategic plans to
become an Amazing City.

Part Three of the book will highlight cities throughout the world and describe some of the ways they are
striving for excellence. There is no perfect city. Cities
are a unique combination of success and failure. Visiting a city without studying its history and its plan for
the future misses an opportunity to learn. The fast pace
of change is requiring cities to take the famous hockey
player, Wayne Gretzky's advice of "skating to where the
puck is going to be, not to where it has been."

As cities look to the future, they will need to be
nimble and resourceful in order to capitalize on the
incredible opportunities available to them. Not every
city will succeed and those without a focus on the needs
of their citizens may fall to the wayside. Cities will need

to find their niche and create a plan to excel in their niche. These are exciting times for cities and with millions of young millennials seeking a great quality of life and millions of Baby Boomers wanting quick access to medical care, entertainment and other services, cities can grow and prosper in Amazing ways!

Part One

7 Steps to Creating an Amazing City

Attitude

"Everything can be taken from a man but one thing: the last of human freedoms - to choose one's attitude in any given set of circumstances, to choose one's own way."
Viktor E. Frankl

How important is a positive attitude in building an Amazing City? More and more, I see examples of people who are turning their communities around and they all have one thing in common, a very positive attitude. When difficulties arise, these people are looking for ways to help and they are the first to volunteer their time and effort to make things better. When you encounter these people, they send out positive vibes and it seems to be infectious. Fellow workers, citizens and visitors all feel the energy and it starts to spread throughout the city.

I often ask my audiences if there is a positive person in their city that they would like me to meet if I visited their city. They will often volunteer a name and immediately a smile appears as they visualize a person who exudes a positive attitude each and every day. I will then ask the audience if there is someone that they would rather me not meet in their town because of that person's poor attitude. This will bring a huge round of laughter as they visualize some grumpy person who brings everyone down.

The responsibility of building a positive attitude is a shared effort. While one person can make a difference, it is so much better when many people join in and assist. It is important for the leadership of the city to be involved and take an active role in spreading a positive message. A positive attitude cannot be imposed on people and often there will be many who actively oppose the efforts to improve the attitude in a community. So often, people like to criticize the city and spread a negative attitude about the community as a way of building themselves up. I've been in restaurants throughout the world and a common discussion at numerous booths is people talking about how bad their community is doing and what fools they have for leaders. While I am sure that this might sometimes be true, constantly spreading negativity does little good in improving a community.

In order to foster a positive attitude, it is important for people to have an idea of the benefits that come with a change in attitude. This is not meant to cover up obvious problems but rather an objective analysis of the strengths and weaknesses in the community. This is often a job for a professional consultant who does not have an investment in the community to avoid bias and preconceived ideas. People do not realize the destructive nature of negativity and sometimes it takes several months or even years to turn around a city that suffered from a constant barrage of negative comments and publicity.

An example of a city that is undergoing a remarkable transformation is the city of Huntington, West Virginia. With a serious drug abuse problem and an economy that is struggling, Mayor Steve Williams of Huntington is working tirelessly to promote a positive attitude for Huntington and it is starting to show results. Huntington recently advanced to the final round of the America's Best Communities competition and is in the running for a top prize of three million dollars. They were also recognized at the West Virginia Municipal League Annual Conference by Thrasher Engineering for the improvement in the city, as well as Mayor Williams receiving the "Mayor of the Year" Award for his efforts in leading the city. While these awards bring resources and positive publicity to the city, the changes in the attitudes of citizens are being seen on social media and other outlets.

There are thousands of examples of people who have changed their communities for the better with a positive attitude. And there is room for as many positive attitudes as can fit in the bounds of the city. When things start to move in a positive direction, the energy increases and growth is exponential. There is a common story that you can talk to the cab driver (or Uber now) from the airport and find out all you need to know about a city. I have found that to be mostly correct.

A positive attitude "will" take your city from great to Amazing!

Motivation

"Wanting something is not enough. You must hunger for it. Your motivation must be absolutely compelling in order to overcome the obstacles that will invariably come your way."
Les Brown

When we look for ways to create an Amazing City, motivation is one of the key components and one that challenges so many people when trying to organize and inspire others to join in. The motivation for many is to improve the lives of others in the community and give back to a community that has blessed them over their lives. I've encountered some people who have a motivation driven by dislike, jealously and underhandedness and their efforts can derail even the most altruistic of souls. The question then becomes, "How can you make a difference in your community when you don't control the various motivations of those involved?" That is an age old question but one that I think is best handled by realizing that it exists.

A city is composed of the supporters as well as the critics and there is no arbitrator that keeps the lines from getting crossed. People's opinions count and for every new apartment building or new baseball park, there are those who would just as soon see things stay as they were. How dissent and conflict is handled is often the determining factor rather than one party being judged as right or wrong. A group of citizens who have joined together to address a drug or crime problem can have great ambitions but if they do not engage the various sectors of the community, their energy and passion may get tied up in petty arguments and dissent. And likewise, when a city decides to put in a public facility such as a jail or group home, not engaging the citizenry is a recipe for disaster. Over my career, I have been amazed at the messes a city can bring upon itself when they forget to engage "all" affected parties to an action.

Often, cities will proceed with projects and initiatives that seem to have little opposition only to learn, late in the process, that there has been a strong undercurrent circulating in the community that had not surfaced. I can remember an instance in my hometown where we were wanting to locate a skateboard park. A local group of teenagers and their parents approached the city council. They found an underused area under a highway overpass that had the room and they had assured us that the neighbors were onboard with this great "civic" project. The council conferred with the park board and found that they were supportive and willing to undertake this project. We investigated the insurance liability issues and the engineering and all were moving along quickly. Since not much activity was occurring on the proposed site, we had no contact from any of the neighbors or businesses.

After several months, construction started. The community excitement was growing with this new addition to our park system. We decided to enforce a time limit on the park so that it would not be open all hours of the night. We felt that vandalism and other issues would be lessened by these rules. We also put in place strict rules on helmets and other safety equipment at the direction of our insurance carrier. This seemed to be acceptable to the teenagers and their parents who were spearheading the park development. All was moving ahead. We had a ribbon cutting with a nice crowd of dignitaries and kids to celebrate a community driven project that would provide an outlet for the "skateboard" crowd who seemed to always be shooed away from plazas and sidewalks in town.

Within a week of the opening, we started to get a rumbling that there were some issues with the skate park. It seemed the skateboard wheels were echoing off the concrete underpass and creating an unbearable "screech" for the residents living nearby. I drove by and had to agree that this would be pretty unbearable if it were next to my house. We decided to look into planting trees or some other obstruction to deaden the noise but unfortunately there were no quick fixes. The kids were oblivious to the complaints and were turning out in record numbers. Quickly things turned bad.

With considerable investment and a community driven project, it became a dueling contest of neighbors against the kids and then against the city. Accusations were being flung about that kids were drinking and doing drugs. Since the park had a closing time, kids would hang around the outside of the park at closing time and take a while to disperse which caused several calls to the police. Just when things started to die down, a young boy was hit by a car outside of the skate park. He had some serious injuries and the calls for the closure of the park increased. The irony of the accident is that the child was not admitted to the park because he did not have the required safety equipment and was heading home at the time of the accident.

Eventually, the park was moved to a new location away from any residents' homes. Although it is more difficult for the young kids to access, it has proven to be a popular attraction and is used regularly throughout the year.

How does this story relate to "motivation"? This is the complex nature of building an Amazing City. The motivation of most everyone involved was positive and the cooperation and community spirit was admirable. Even the neighbors wanted only to enjoy their property in a peaceful and quiet manner. I think the lesson learned was that it is important to not take silence as approval or to take opposition as counter to community support. Listening and seeing the issue from various points of view is critical and can help avoid numerous confrontations. When motivation is analyzed and found to be in the community's best interest, even the largest obstacles can be overcome.

Famed Notre Dame Football coach, Lou Holtz is quoted as saying, "Ability is what you're capable of doing. Motivation determines what you do. Attitude determines how well you do it." I think this captures the heart of how motivation fits into the puzzle in creating an Amazing City. Just because someone approaches things differently or has a conflicting point of view is not evidence of a lack of motivation or worse yet, destructive motivation. It is necessary to examine the various points of view and see if there can be a solution that takes in the concerns of all. Inevitably, this will not work in all situations but a transparent process with an open and constructive manner will often succeed, even when some people's needs are not met.

The rewards are so great that it is worth the effort to hit the ground running to inspire and motivate citizens, employees, businesses and others to make their city Amazing.

Attention to Detail

"A man's accomplishments in life are the cumulative effect of his attention to detail."
John Foster Dulles

My father, Rex Hunt, worked for the City of Clarksburg, West Virginia Public Works Department as a heavy equipment operator during my childhood and college years. When he would come home from work, he would talk about his workday and what projects he was working on. He took pride in his job and would sometimes take us down obscure alleys on our Sunday outings after church. Many times he would point out the perfectly laid gravel and the clean ditch lines that he had worked on the previous week. I don't know if the residents knew the care that went into a job that many would look at as menial and unimportant. He would often see street signs out of place or vandalized and the following week they would be repaired.

I must have inherited my father's attention to detail. During my elected tenure as Mayor and Councilmember in my hometown, I would note dozens of items that would be turned into the City Manager for attention. Often I would check out the work and request that they revisit the job and tidy it up. Some might call this obsessive but I believe that attention to detail is as critical to becoming an Amazing City as any other trait. Overflowing garbage cans and weeds growing out of the sidewalks can doom a downtown or neighborhood. Out of control trees and shrubs often block sidewalks, forcing citizens to step into the street and eventually causing them to avoid an area entirely. Cities often install signs and traffic control devices for construction projects and fail to remove them long after the construction is complete.

City vehicles also need attention to detail as they are the visible "brand" of the city traveling throughout the streets each day. Fleet management might seem to some a frivolous exercise but look at successful businesses that maintain spotless vehicles with consistent signage and paint colors. A city can send an important message to both citizens and visitors alike: that they care about their image. Code officials and others who interact with the public can gain important credibility by presenting a professional image to the public. Far too often we have allowed poorly marked vehicles with poorly dressed employees to communicate a silent message of indifference to those they interact with daily.

I have visited city buildings throughout the world. The ones that pay attention to detail are the ones that seem to be on everyone's "best city" list. Before you shout out that "this takes money and it's easy to pay attention to detail when you are financially well off", let me say this: my experiences tend to counter this. Some of the wealthiest cities in the country are the worst examples of clean, well-kept cities. I stood on the 8th floor of the City Hall in a major American city, looking at a $200-million-dollar riverfront improvement project and was appalled at the boarded up buildings and broken sidewalks with weeds growing through them leading up to this "marquis" development in this major city. And, I have visited poverty ridden towns with immaculate sidewalks and well maintained parks with smiling children swinging and playing. The key is the attention to detail paid by citizens and city officials alike.

On a National League of Cities trip to St. Petersburg, Florida, Mayor Rick Baker was giving us a tour of the city and stopped the bus next to a subsidized housing development. Mayor Baker took out his phone and stepped off the bus. When he got back on, he said, "That broken screen will be taken care of tomorrow." That is Attention to Detail!

People often tell me that the reason their towns look so slipshod and disheveled is that "those" people just don't care. Well, the job of creating an Amazing City is everyone's job. It is a culture that is developed from the bottom up and the top down. It is the Mayor that picks up litter on his way into City Hall. It is the citizen who carries a trash bag on their morning walk and picks up the fast food wrappers and cups. It is the neighborhood groups who organize weekend cleanups and it is the city officials who coordinate with these groups to remove the trash in a quick and efficient manner. Businesses play a critical role and can assist by being good corporate citizens and supporting a beautification effort in downtowns and neighborhoods.

The effort is certainly not easy but once it becomes part of a city's culture, you will be surprised at how projects materialize from thin air. In most city halls across the country, youth groups are constantly asking the city to fund travel or recognitions for sport or educational efforts. An Amazing City will celebrate these youth groups but may request that in exchange for the city's support, that the team join the Mayor and other city officials on a Saturday to clean up a park or paint fence posts or similar jobs. This win-win approach creates energy in a city and promotes more creative efforts in the future.

The average city has their largest investment in city buildings, parks, roads, utilities and other holdings. Letting these important assets be overtaken by neglect is wasteful and gives a very poor image of the city. It also sends out an unspoken message to the residents that "if the city keeps its property looking like crap, it should be ok for us!" Amazing cities can point with pride at their facilities and rightly demand that citizens keep that same attention to detail on their properties. For those who might disagree with this assessment, I would ask that you visit your local fast food hangout on any Saturday morning. I am placing money that you will hear this sentiment expressed by the members of the early morning coffee club.

I can hear some people grumbling as you read these words that this is fine in small town America but it doesn't work in the "Big City". Let me introduce you to Councilmember Joe Buscaino, a Councilmember in Los Angeles, California. Joe has instilled attention to detail in his district and is having remarkable results. He regularly organizes cleanups and neighborhood celebrations. Once-dilapidated neighborhoods are showing signs of life. Kids are seeing that they can make a difference in their neighborhood and enjoy clean parks and graffiti free areas. Joe uses Facebook, Twitter and other forms of social media to organize and advertise his events. And Joe Buscaino is not alone in this effort. Matt Zone, a Councilmember in Cleveland, Ohio has transformed his district into one of the most interesting and exciting in the country through his attention to detail and neighborhood empowerment. There are countless examples of cities and neighborhoods prospering and becoming Amazing throughout the country.

The consistent theme among them is their obsessive "ATTENTION TO DETAIL".

Developing this new culture is one that requires consistency and commitment. Citizens need to feel empowered to be creative and organize grass root events. City officials need to participate and take a hands-on approach without trying to take over the effort. Surprisingly, there is more than enough exposure to go around. Success is infectious with even bigger and better projects being suggested.

"Zing"

"There's beauty everywhere. There are amazing things happening everywhere, you just have to be able to open your eyes and witness it. Some days, that's harder than others."
Sarah McLachlan

As I began my speaking career, the business book, *Good to Great: Why Some Companies Make the Leap...and Others Don't* was topping all the best seller lists. I liked the premise and found some great insight in this book but for some reason, it just didn't convey my passion for instilling excellence in municipal government. I was driving to Washington, DC one day for a meeting and kept going over and over, trying to find a word that fit the message that I was developing. Suddenly, a news story was on the radio and a young child was telling the story of seeing an elephant for the first time at the zoo and he blurted out, "It was Amazing!" I knew in that minute that I had found my word. I didn't want to just go from good to great, I wanted 'freaking' Amazing!

Amazing is such a powerful word and describes a feeling of sheer joy better than any other word. Children use it frequently when opening a gift or seeing a rainbow or riding a rollercoaster. It excites the listener and makes them wish that they were there. When Michael Phelps is asked what it feels like to win a gold medal, he regularly uses the word "Amazing". When you arrive on the rim of the Grand Canyon, the echo that is heard most often is, "This is Amazing!" Why should we not want our communities to be Amazing? Why should we settle for ok when such a powerful word as Amazing is hanging out there, begging to be used?

The more I used the word, the more it resonated with my audiences and readers. The acronym that you are following in this chapter developed naturally when I put together the keys to creating an Amazing City but I drew a blank when trying to find a word that began with "Z". I consulted numerous dictionaries and could not find an appropriate word. As I searched, the thing that I most wanted to convey was that singular thing that makes a city Amazing. The Eiffel Tower in Paris, the Washington Monument in DC, the hanging flowers in Fairhope, Alabama or the Golden Gate Bridge in San Francisco. I came up with "Zing" because it is somewhat undefinable but you know exactly what it is when you see it. It is that thing that stands out among everything and makes your city unique.

This sometimes confuses my audiences since they will point out that there are many things that make their communities unique and it is impossible to narrow it down to one. While I somewhat agree with their assessment, in this fast paced world, it is necessary to focus in order to catch the attention of the public. Businesses have done this for years and when a company succeeds like Nike with their "Swoosh" or McDonald's with their "Golden Arches", it is pure gold. In this digital world, we have a scant few seconds to impress our uniqueness on our visitors and citizens. When we present a confusing message or image, we stand to lose the eyeballs of the public. If you are driving through Georgia and you happen upon the huge water tower shaped like a peach, do you need a better 'brand' to attract visitors? The small town of Olney, Illinois has become famous for being the home of the "White Squirrels". It is hard to walk a block without being reminded of their "Zing" through an effective array of signage and promotional materials. While the city of Olney has many fine attributes in addition to the White Squirrels, they have created a worldwide identity that causes many a visitor to turn off the highway and spend some of their dollars in the city.

Finding your "Zing" is a helpful exercise to engage citizens, businesses and others to help define what your unique brand is. Even if everyone is not on the exact same page, the discussion might bring out some things that have been overlooked or are no longer relevant to the current generation. A city that stakes claim as the birthplace of an obscure athlete, long forgotten by most, may find more traction with having the claim to fame of an *America's Got Talent* contestant. The small town of Logan, West Virginia did just that with Landau Murphy, Jr. Murphy, the winner of season six of the show has put the town of Logan on the map and his concerts feature him talking affectionately of his hometown.

The "Zing" can be a thing, a place, a person or event. It can be known throughout the world or just in your region or state. It can change over time or it can be as timeless as the *Mona Lisa*. The idea is to interject energy and excitement in the process and put a smile on the faces of citizens and visitors alike. Can you imagine the number of photos of the Rocky statue that have been taken in front of the Philadelphia Museum of Art in Philadelphia, Pennsylvania or the people who have recreated that famous run up the 72 steps of the now famous "Rocky Steps"?

On a business trip to Albuquerque, New Mexico, my

traveling buddy, Brian Davis asked me what I wanted to see. Since we had a few hours, I said that I wanted to see the A-1 Carwash made famous in the television series *Breaking Bad*. Brian and I did a Google search and navigated to the landmark and dutifully took our pictures in front of the carwash. On the ride over, we got to see the heart of Albuquerque and appreciated the beautiful Southwest architecture of the buildings and the numerous restaurants. After enjoying a wonderful New Mexico lunch, we remarked as to how we might have missed a lot of the city had we not had the *Breaking Bad* experience. Not everyone will include the A-1 Carwash as their "Zing" but it has become a regular stop for thousands of visitors to Albuquerque.

Inclusiveness

"I have a dream that my four little children will one day live in a nation where they will not be judged by the color of their skin, but by the content of their character."
Martin Luther King, Jr.

Traditionally, when someone is elected as 2nd Vice-President of the National League of Cities, they would identify a topic to use as their Presidential Initiative. Over the next two years, the NLC Staff and the NLC Advisory Council would research and develop the topic and a program would be developed to be rolled out during the President's year. Experts on the topic would be invited to meetings and committees assigned to dissect the topic and come up with ideas to implement. Over the years, NLC Presidents had identified topics like budgeting, infrastructure and the like for research and review. Early in my elected career, Mayor Bob Knight of Wichita, Kansas chose "Undoing Racism" as his Presidential topic. Mayor Knight was a white, Republican Mayor and he made an indelible mark on me as a public official. He would often remark that when he told people about his chosen topic, he would get many strange looks.

Mayor Knight led the National League of Cities through an important period in the organization's history. As more and more African-American and Hispanic officials were elected to office, people began to question the inclusiveness of the organization. The officers of the organization were exclusively white until Mayor Tom

Bradley of Los Angeles was selected in 1974. It was 1986 before San Antonio Mayor Henry Cisneros became the first Hispanic president of the organization. It was 1977 when Councilwoman Phyllis Lamphere of Seattle, Washington broke the gender barrier and in 1980, Councilwoman Jessie M. Rattley of Newport News, Virginia became the first African-American woman to hold the post of president.

Mayor Knight knew that if America's cities were to address the difficult issue of racism, he might be able to bridge the gap and provide a dialog to pull some of the reluctant white officials into the discussion. The discussions were tense at times and voices were often raised. Meetings would go far past their scheduled times. Discussions would often carry over to the bars and restaurants till the late hours of the evening. During this time, my city of Clarksburg, West Virginia was having its own racial issues. With the election of the first African-American Mayor, the Ku Klux Klan planned a rally in the downtown district of the city. Pastor David D.A. Kates, a Baptist minister, was elected to city council and at his first meeting, was elected Mayor from amongst his peers. Pastor Kates was a unique individual. He decided to approve the permit for the Klan rally but he also vowed to rally the community at a local park.

Pastor Kates asked me to assist him with the rally. We quickly put together an eclectic group of speakers and performers to rally on a cold, October afternoon. The rally gained statewide attention and preparations were made to protect the city from violence or disruption. After much media attention and fanfare, the Ku Klux Klan rally was relatively peaceful with some shouting and name calling. The Unity Rally turned out to be a huge gathering of a diverse group of people singing and talking about ways to bring the community together. This led to a series of community meetings and presentations to local schools that put Mayor Kates on a national stage as a spokesperson for unity and diversity. He won a national award given by the National Black Mayors Association and he and I were invited to Caux, Switzerland to present to an international gathering of city officials.

Throughout this period, the National League of Cities continued to address racial diversity and inclusiveness in America's cities. South Bay, Florida Mayor Clarence Anthony followed Mayor Knight's lead and continued the presidential topic to explore more aspects of the nation's growing diversity. NLC President, Alderman Charlie Lyons from Arlington, Massachusetts addressed the growing inequity in America's cities and appointed me to chair the NLC Advisory Council leading the study. When I was elected as 2nd Vice-President of the National League of Cities in 2003, it seemed natural to bring the growing body of research together. My presidential topic was proposed to be "Building a Nation of Inclusive Communities".

Little did I know the journey we would travel on the road to implementing this body of work. We convened several national meetings to bring in experts to discuss the issue and propose strategies for implementation. One presenter, in particular, talked about the cost of the current path of incarcerating young black males and its lifelong impact on our society. Harvard professor, Dr. Charles Ogletree is one of the nation's leading experts on minority incarceration. He held the audience spellbound during his remarks.

As 2006 approached, we had decided to begin a national program that cities would need to join to develop individual strategies to implement an inclusive agenda. I appointed Mayor Steve Burkholder of Lakewood, Colorado to chair the Advisory Council. They did a great job developing the program. While we offered suggestions and proposed exercises, the individual communities were tasked with developing their own programs to meet their specific needs. This led to over 190 cities joining the effort with over 19 million citizens represented. A visible symbol of the program was a large sign that was placed at the entrances of the participating cities. The sign stated, "Welcome-We Are Building an Inclusive Community." The message was well thought out and made it clear that this is an ongoing effort. The process of inclusiveness does not end with a Mayor or city council's term but rather continues on as a part of the culture of the city.

Future NLC President, Mayor Ted Ellis of Bluffton, Indiana was featured in a front page story in USA Today about his efforts to create a more inclusive environment in his city. Numerous other media coverage gave the program exposure and the large signs were being placed throughout the country.

Why Inclusiveness? With a growing diversity in the United States and unresolved issues from decades before, it is hard to be truly Amazing without addressing inclusiveness. Many cities have found that they have all of the components to be successful but they are continually falling short of Amazing. Conversely, cities who have made inclusiveness a core part of their community have seen a growing economy and a sense of working together that strengthens the fabric of the city.

Not surprisingly, the technology sector and the Millennial generation have come to expect inclusiveness. When it is not present they will vote with their feet. Even remote towns and villages have found that welcoming those who might look a little different than they do can be a strategy for new jobs and exciting developments that are sustainable and long lasting. Several small towns in Virginia and West Virginia have benefitted from a diverse array of people who have escaped the beltway of Washington, DC and created thousands of jobs and revitalized decades old buildings as they realize that a slower paced lifestyle is quite attractive when communities adopt an inclusive approach.

As we look to the future, inclusiveness may well mark the divide between success and failure in cities. Cities who fail to address racial, gender and sexual orientation issues may find themselves excluded from the new economy and opportunities that are available in a diverse society. An entire generation of adults have little memory of a segregated society or a time when people were openly discriminated against. While there are many issues to work on, cities who are failing to plan will most certainly be planning to fail. It is hard to imagine the word Amazing being used to describe a city that is defined by unresolved racism, sexism or other forms of discrimination.

Cities can reach out to organizations like the National League of Cities for resources to assist in implementing an inclusive agenda. This does not guarantee that a community is not beset by a tragic event or an incident of hatred, but communities that have had a history of coming together during peaceful times are often better prepared in times of crisis.

I am so proud of the National League of Cities and the efforts that they have made to become one of the most inclusive organizations in the United States. A special highlight of my time at NLC was seeing NLC President Marie Lopez Rogers sitting with First Lady, Michele Obama at the State of the Union Address. President Obama related Marie's story of picking cotton as a migrant farm worker on the same land where she served as Mayor at the Avondale, Arizona City Hall.

Mayor Bob Knight did a great service for his city and his country by beginning a discussion of difficult issues that continues to this day. His legacy has an unbroken chain of inclusiveness at the National League of Cities. Their leadership has provided thousands of public officials and their citizens a path to inclusiveness and an Amazing future.

Neighborhood Empowerment

"If you don't visit the bad neighborhoods, the bad neighborhoods are going to visit you."
Thomas Friedman

I grew up in the Montpelier neighborhood in Clarksburg, West Virginia. It was composed of an area of town
that was separated from most of the city by a series of
railroad tracks. It had a small store and a restaurant
named "The Corner Lunch". The Montpelier playground
was the central place for kids. We grew up playing basketball and generally hanging around the swing sets
and teeter totters until darkness fell or someone heard
your mother yelling for you to get home. There were
several industrial buildings and a Royal Crown Cola
bottling plant where you could collect empty bottles and
trade them for twenty or thirty cents a case. The homes
were small and I cannot remember ever spending the
night at another friend's house. You knew everyone
in the neighborhood. When a truck would show up at
an empty house, you would sit around watching them
unload their belongings and seeing if they had kids and
jealously checking out a new sled or a shiny bicycle.

The neighborhood seemed to work just fine. Once a
summer, all of the families would bring a covered dish to
the park and spend a pleasant evening sharing stories
and recipes. The Democratic committeewoman kept a
close eye on everything political. Election season would

bring the occasional new sidewalk or a strip of freshly laid asphalt. If there was a bicycle missing or an egg splattered on a car, the local police officer would quickly visit the local delinquent. The bike would be returned and a forced apology given. Drugs were nonexistent and beer was generally introduced to teens on a hot summer day by their fathers, who were soon to be admonished by their wives.

As I grew up and entered local politics, I realized that the neighborhood experience existed throughout the city with little variance. Oh, the richer parts of town had better basketball courts and some even had the luxury of extra tall sliding boards and splash pools but generally they were quite similar. Our little city could not operate without these neatly divided little enclaves and it all worked pretty well. For many years I believed that growing up in a neighborhood was limited to small towns in rural areas and that the 'big city' experience was fundamentally different.

I shared this with my good friend, Alderman Joe Moore of Chicago and he laughed. "Chicago is just a lot of different neighborhoods that work pretty much like West Virginia, but there are just a lot more of them," he explained. I started to realize that virtually all cities are composed of neighborhoods and they play a critical role in the ability to govern and provide services to the residents. Neighborhoods help new residents get adjusted to the city and can provide a lot of social capital to aid families and others in need of assistance.

Can a city be Amazing without empowering their neighborhoods and harnessing the power of these quasi-government units? I don't think so. Empowered neighborhoods can serve a valued role in organizing citizens and interacting with government. An empowered neighborhood can be a healthy training ground for citizens who want to improve the quality of life in a city. It can also serve as a sounding board for community issues and give citizens a way to have their voice heard on important decisions.

A couple of years ago, I stopped into Cleveland, Ohio Councilmember Matt Zone's district office and it was abuzz with activity. I asked Matt if it was always that busy and he said that it was. Matt said, "People look to the office to connect with city staff and sometimes just to stop and chat." Matt has figured out that keeping a finger on the pulse of the neighborhood is a good idea and provides an insight that is often impossible to get at City Hall.

Technology has also given neighborhoods several new tools to assist in becoming Amazing. Social media is giving neighborhoods a way of organizing and communicating that exceeds anything available in my little hillside neighborhood of years ago. Recently, a family in my town posted a security video of a teen stealing a bike from a neighbor's porch. The crime was solved by the neighbors on Facebook and the bike was returned the following day. Creative app developers are working on more enhanced products that can bring neighbors together in a way that will make organizing and improving the neighborhoods much easier.

On occasion, I have talked to some city officials who are not enamored with the idea of empowering neighborhoods. They are fearful of increased calls for service and a breeding ground for political opposition. This fear can often have the opposite effect. Those officials who block empowerment efforts are sometimes swept out of office and replaced by those who have connected in the neighborhood, rolled up their sleeves and went to work.

When neighborhoods work, cities work! An Amazing neighborhood can enhance a community and improve the quality of life in Amazing cities. Whether it be a large city with hundreds of interconnected, empowered neighborhoods or a small town with one or two neighborhoods, neighborhood empowerment can be the catalyst to an Amazing City. When in doubt, be Amazing!

Green Awareness

"Harmony with land is like harmony with a friend; you cannot cherish his right hand and chop off his left."
Aldo Leopold

Cities throughout the world are leading a remarkable movement to conserve energy and clean up the planet after centuries of abuse to the environment. Innovative programs have been developed and cities have worked with public and private entities to install energy efficient lighting and other building improvements. Hundreds of thousands of LED streetlights are going up in cities throughout the world. Energy contracting companies have entered into performance contracts to install upgrades to heating and cooling units at little cost to the cities. Clean drinking water is being recognized as a dwindling resource and cities have invested billions of dollars to install conservation enhancements to their water plants.

Citizens have also stepped up to the plate by participating in recycling programs and passing initiatives to fund many energy efficient programs. Schools have developed lesson plans around ecology. The vast majority of schools recycle a high percentage of their solid waste. Compost facilities are increasing and a growing number of citizens send yard waste to the compost facilities and will likewise pick up truckloads of rich compost to assist with gardens and lawns.

While this has been encouraging, there is so much more to do. Electronic equipment, medical waste and toxic substances such as contaminated water pose huge problems for many communities with little revenue streams to fund disposal and cleanup. Cities are finding big screen television sets showing up on abandoned lots and dead end streets. Other substances are routinely dumped into rivers and streams.

Moving forward, it will be hard to be an Amazing City without a strategic plan to address these issues. My good friend and former City Manager, Mike Conduff, regularly tells me that more education is needed before citizens recognize the tragic consequences that befall our cities. Landfill permits are becoming increasingly difficult to obtain and space is becoming scarce. While citizens look at thousands of acres of adjacent farmland to their city and wonder why we don't just open up a few hundred more acres, the reality is that modern solid waste disposal is reliant on a reduction in waste stream in order to be cost affordable.

I recently visited Councilwoman Shirley Scott of Tucson, Arizona at her LEED certified district council office and was so impressed at the leadership she is providing on the environmental front. Shirley walked me through the building and knowledgably explained the components of the building and how they worked to conserve energy and water. An Amazing City will walk the walk and talk the talk on energy issues and provide a model for citizens to follow.

Former St. Petersburg, Florida Mayor Rick Baker is another official who found that leading the way on energy and water conservation was good for the city's bottom line. Rick wrote about his efforts in his popular book, *The Seamless City* and is still enthusiastic about his use of LED lighting and reducing the pollution of precious drinking water. A prominent Republican, Mayor Baker also proved that green awareness is not a partisan issue but rather one that can appeal to the most conservative of citizens.

In talking to dozens of leading Mayors around the world, it becomes clear that the first step in any "green initiative" is to bring citizens to the table and work with them to develop a well thought out plan. Most large cities and many smaller cities are hiring a director of green programs and empowering them to enact changes throughout the city. The biggest challenge for many of these "green managers" is that they quickly become overwhelmed with the multitude of facilities and aspects of the city operations. They often find themselves focusing on a smaller list of items that they would like. This is why planning is important to get the "low hanging fruit" taken care of before moving on to larger and more time consuming ventures.

Technology is helping and the amount of innovative solutions for energy conservation is growing every day. I recently met with a gentleman who had developed a patented switch for massive motors that would analyze the electric needs and efficiently allocate the electric, resulting in a 33 percent savings. The switch was about the size of a deck of cards and could be installed in less than a day. The previously mentioned LED lighting continues to improve and much of the new innovations are around the control of the lighting. With "Smart" technology, streetlights can stay dim until a motion sensor detects movement causing the lights to increase in brightness. The color rendering is also improving and lighting is becoming programmable to address the needs of shopping areas and neighborhoods alike.

Solar lighting is becoming more efficient. The ability to have light in remote park areas and trails without installing expensive electric lines is opening up public space that was previously cost prohibitive. Residents and visitors also embrace these improvements and a most often heard remark is, "That's Amazing!"

Think about the value of operating your city with a fraction of the electric, gas and water that you are currently using. Citizens are seeing energy efficient vehicles driving on city streets and being plugged into an outlet at City Hall. We are only beginning to see the promise of energy conservation and a respect for our planet. When there is abundant water to provide to growing businesses and housing developments, your competitive advantage increases. Your citizens benefit with a higher quality of life and lower cost of living.

The need for cities to play a leadership role in the "green" movement is crucial. National strategies get bogged down in politics and often the proponents and opponents use fuzzy math to extol their positions. The value of cities is that we can deliver real time numbers on real time projects. And, while some projects may fail, it will serve as a learning tool for other cities without bankrupting the system. The recent water conservation project in Los Angeles using millions of round plastic "shade" balls to prevent evaporation was not as successful as first thought but they gave thousands of cities an innovative way of looking at conservation. The unique needs of Los Angeles prevented using the balls on some of the water reservoirs but the publicity reached around the world in just a few days. Scientists and water engineers were given a new way of looking at an age old problem.

I am often reminded of a story I heard about a city in southern West Virginia that discovered a water leak in one of their parks. The line was relatively small and it was broken near a small stream that ran through the park. When the pipe was repaired, the city received the next month's water bill which had reduced over $3,000. They thought it was a mistake since the water bill was consistent for the past five or so years. What they found was that the water line running into the stream had been leaking for over five years straight, twenty-four hours a day, costing the city over $150,000 that they could see. Green Awareness is a lot like that water line. It is dollars that are being wasted through inefficiency and wastefulness, but because we have become accustomed to it, we don't seem to notice it.

An Amazing City will provide the education and leadership to provide a model for their citizens to build a more sustainable future. The rewards will be large and small and they will accrue to our children and grandchildren. One day, a little kid will look back and say, "I think my grandparents are just Amazing!" Isn't that why we do this?

Part Two

Ideas for Building Amazing Cities

A Bright Light in Your Future!

"When Thomas Edison worked late into the night on the electric light, he had to do it by gas lamp or candle. I'm sure it made the work seem that much more urgent."
George Carlin

A big change is happening in America. It is one that will be coming to your town in the near future. LED street lighting is changing the look and feel of cities. It is a change for the better. There is probably nothing that gives you a feeling of safety and security as a well-lit city street. Criminals tend to avoid streets that are properly illuminated. Businesses flourish when customers can park and enjoy their services without the danger of dark corners and shadowy storefronts. Unfortunately, with tight budgets and rising electric costs, many cities have reduced public lighting and found it harder and harder to adequately light their downtowns and neighborhood streets. Well, help is coming and it is primarily due to advances in energy efficient lighting and technology to control how the lights operate.

Street lighting has a unique history in America. It began in Philadelphia, Pennsylvania when Benjamin Franklin invented a unique four-sided lamp that had a candle which was lit each evening by a lamplighter. That system was used in many cities and remained until 1803 when gas lights were introduced to Pelham Street in Newport, Rhode Island and the city of Baltimore. The use of gas lights spread throughout the country and remarkably, some are still in use today. When inventor, Thomas Edison pioneered the use of electricity, street lights were developed to take advantage of this "new" technology. The first city in America to use electric street lights was Wabash, Indiana when the city council approved a test of the lights in 1880.

Over the years, electric streetlights saw acceptance throughout the United States and most citizens came to expect lighting as part of their city services. The type of streetlights also evolved and went from using large incandescent bulbs that were often the target of teenage boys with BB guns to mercury vapor and high and low pressure sodium bulbs. Mercury vapor was outlawed due to the use of mercury and the sodium bulbs, while popular, cast a amber colored light that many citizens feel do not adequately light up the streets. Metal Halide, Induction and Fluorescent lights are also used in street lighting with varying success. Electric cost is also a growing concern. Many cities are spending hundreds of thousands of dollars each year while citizens keep requesting the installation of additional lights throughout the city.

This led to the development of a new type of streetlight. Light Emitting Diode or LED lighting is showing up in more and more cities and has a promising future as a long-life, energy efficient form of lighting. LED street lights cast a 'white' light and have excellent color rendering ability that "light up" city streets and enable good clarity for security cameras that are in use in many cities. The lights can also be fitted with controllers that adjust the color and detect motion to increase the light when traffic or pedestrians are present and dim during inactivity. Side by side comparisons are dramatic. More and more citizens are realizing the value of having this new technology in their city.

The question might be asked why all cities are not rushing to this new lighting technology. The big challenge is cost. The upfront investment is daunting to cities faced with tight budgets and declining revenues. Fortunately, because of the energy efficiency of this new lighting technology, many cities are exploring ways to pay for the lights through the energy savings. This may speed up the adoption rate within the United States.

While street lighting might not seem to be that exciting, for cities that want to stand out, be innovative and save money, these new lights can truly make your city an AMAZING City!

City Council-
City Manager Relations

"Good management is the art of making problems so interesting and their solutions so constructive that everyone
wants to get to work and deal with them."
Paul Hawken

Each year I speak with thousands of city officials. One
of the topics that seems to be near the top of the
list are issues surrounding city council-city manager
relationships. A healthy council-manager relationship
is critical to the success of a city. A dysfunctional relationship can often adversely affect the city staff and the
interaction with citizens. There are many reasons why
council-manager relationships are difficult but often
they can be improved by analyzing some of the dynam-
ics of the relationship.

Failure to communicate is often cited as the beginning
of a breakdown in the council-manager relationship. In
today's busy times, city managers will often use text mes-
saging or email to communicate with their city council,
without finding out if all members of council prefer to
communicate in that manner. Some city managers use
written memos and reports to distribute information
and that might infuriate a councilmember who would
rather receive a quick text or email. How can a manager
win? One tip is to discuss a communication strategy
with the governing body and decide on a method that
works for everyone. Be considerate of everyone and if

there is a need to accommodate a member, it is a good idea to do so. Many city councils are using laptops or IPads to distribute information. If a member is not a technology user, communication issues may be looming in the future.

Some might think that a city manager needs a Doctorate in Psychology to do their job. While that might be helpful, it is important to understand the personalities and needs of their councilmembers. Often, problems arise when new members join a council and they feel out of the loop because veteran councilmembers seem to have a closer relationship with the manager. In my 27-year career, I often counseled fellow councilmembers that it takes a while to develop a good relationship and feel comfortable with the manager. Many times they formed a negative opinion for reasons that were not the fault of the city manager but just a difference in personalities.

I think one of the most important factors in establishing a good city council-city manager relationship is to recognize the unique properties of the city manager form of government. In it, a professional manager is appointed by a governing body to run the city while the council oversees the budget and policy making responsibilities of the city. Too many times, councilmembers fail to respect the boundaries of their city charter and overstep into duties that are in the domain of the manager. Likewise, some managers will attempt to legislate or control the budget, often with disastrous results.

My good friend, Mike Conduff, a former board member of the International City Managers Association (ICMA) and City Manager in several cities in Texas and Kansas, often kids me about who is at fault in a dysfunctional council-manager relationship. I tell Mike that if city managers would just follow the advice of mayors and councilmembers, that all would be right with the world! Mike smiles but has never really given me an answer on that one.

City Websites

"City websites are the new welcome signs in a digital world."
Jim Hunt

With the advent of the Internet, cities have a new and exciting way to connect with citizens and visitors. When people are thinking about moving to a new city, their first visit is, more often than not, made via the internet rather than an in person visit. Likewise, when businesses are looking to expand into a new city or area, they also will visit the city online. This gives smaller cities the ability to compete with their larger neighbors and often can make the difference between getting a new resident or business.

Many citizens use the internet to interact with City Hall and will often pay tickets or obtain permits without making a trip there. They can also view city council meetings and committee meetings along with viewing agendas and minutes. This is extremely helpful to citizens that have children or work schedules that prohibit them from attending in person. As technology has advanced, it is relativity easy to record and store video and make it available online.

Social media is also becoming a good way for cities to disseminate information about events or emergency situations. Facebook, Twitter and YouTube are a cost effective way to provide information and allows all ages of citizens to communicate with city hall. Many elected officials maintain individual social media accounts and are able to interact with citizens and respond to problems immediately from anywhere in the world. There is a need for the city to establish good policies regarding social media and keep tabs on the accounts but this is becoming more standardized and generally problem free.

While larger cities employ social media managers and video production technicians, smaller cities can look to volunteers, interns or part-time employees to establish a footing on the world-wide-web. Many small cities have high-quality websites and social media presence due to the work of a dedicated employee who enjoys working with technology and has a desire to see their city represented on the web.

The availability of broadband is another issue that impacts many cities throughout the country, primarily in rural areas. When a community does not have high speed internet service available, it impacts residents and businesses alike. Many people can operate businesses from their homes but only if they are able to stream video and connect to their company's servers.

I recently did a survey of West Virginia cities to see if they had websites and were using social media in their communities. Surprisingly, over 100 cities in West Virginia do not have a website and many more have inferior sites that do not offer even the basic services needed in today's world. The economic impact of this lack of web presence is hard to calculate but it is significant.

We live in a digital world and it is important to make sure that cities are up to date with technology. Each month, another innovation is announced that can help cities save energy and protect their citizens. In order to take advantage of these exciting technologies, we need high speed broadband and we need cities to lead the way.

Community Oriented Government

"Citizenship consists in the service of the country."
Jawaharlal Nehru

Many years ago, I met the Mayor of Fort Wayne, Indiana. He opened my eyes to a new way of looking at local government. His name was Paul Helmke. I have been a disciple ever since I met him. His theory was that every citizen is responsible for the quality of their own government and they need to do their part with support from the city. Not everyone wants to run for city council or take a leadership role in the community. As people are busy with their jobs and family responsibilities, often there is little time left to make an impact in the community. Another reason that people do not join in on many projects is that they are not sure what they are allowed to do in a city and what might be prohibited. I've put together a list of five things that citizens can do and can really make a difference in a community.

Picking up litter: While this seems obvious, many people will walk by litter on their street and complain that the city is a mess. This is a task that can be done by individuals, groups and even families. When you walk your dog, carry a garbage bag with you and pick up the bottles and paper that are on the sidewalk and in the street. If you bring an old plastic grocery bag for your dog, bring an extra one to protect your hands. You will be surprised how much you can pick up and it will not be long before you see less and less litter on your street.

Cleaning Utility Poles: With hundreds of yard sales, garage sales and birthday party announcements being stapled, nailed and taped to utility poles, taking an hour or so to remove the staples and tape can make the neighborhood look better while making the poles safer for the utility workers who climb them. Take a small plastic bucket with a flat screwdriver and a pair of pliers. Most of the staples will pop right out but some may need the leverage of the screwdriver. Snap a picture of the pole before you start to work and take one afterwards. Posting the pictures on social media might encourage people to be more careful when posting these signs. Doing this really does help the utility workers since they are often required to climb the poles in bad weather when they may not see the nails and staples and could cut themselves quite badly.

Painting Sign Posts: The street signs in many cities have sign posts that have become rusted and unsightly. A little black paint can make a difference in the appearance of these poles. I've painted the signs in front of my office and on my street and it gives a clean and neat look. Don't get creative and use pink or orange paint since that may be frowned on by the city but it's hard to go wrong with black paint. Most times it only takes thirty minutes or less and often you can do several while you have your brush and paint at the ready.

Graffiti Removal: Cities have a crisis with the amount of graffiti that seems to be everywhere. Mailboxes, walls, buildings and garbage dumpsters are frequent targets. It gives the neighborhood a very bad look and seems to encourage more and more graffiti. When I worked in the Sunnyside neighborhood in Morgantown, West Virginia, we had groups of students who would paint the dump-sters. We ended up painting over one hundred in all. It really made a difference and since we used the blue and gold colors of WVU, everyone seemed to like it.

Trimming Overgrown Shrubs: Many sidewalks in a city have so much overgrown brush and trees growing into the right-a-way that people are unable to walk on the sidewalk. You have to be careful not to trim some-one's prize planting, but generally, you can tell the overgrown things that are blocking the walks.

Always be careful when working on these projects and if possible, give the city a heads up. You might even get the city to agree to pick up the piles of brush or bags of garbage. If one idea does not work, try another. There are so many ways to improve your community that you shouldn't run out of things to do. And remember, use social media like Facebook and Twitter to encour-age others to follow your example. In just a few short months you can see the difference and be well on your way to becoming an Amazing City!

Downtown Redevelopment

"I grew up in the suburbs, so I figured 'Why not try downtown living?' And, honestly, I love it. I've been very pleasantly surprised at how much downtown Indianapolis has to offer."
Andrew Luck, NFL Quarterback

When you look at old photographs of cities, you see the ways in which they have changed over the years. It is not always evident when you live in that city, but with the passage of time, you see how cities reinvent themselves. At one time, automobiles competed with horse drawn wagons for parking space and many cities still have the remnants of water troughs and "hitching" posts. Mass transportation has also changed with more people in cars and less people relying on buses and street cars. Many cities demolished old storefronts to make way for the influx of cars. This led to a need for businesses to build standalone buildings with large parking lots for their customers.

Downtowns used to be the center of the community and few businesses could survive if they were located out of the core 'business' zone of a city. Likewise, housing was often clustered close to factories and other employment centers as employees needed to live close to their work. This led to people living next to steel factories belching out black smoke and kids playing in slag piles or near noisy machinery that operated twenty-four hours a day. Few complaints were lodged since people needed the jobs and being close seemed to be an asset to the employees.

Housing was built very close together to facilitate the installation of water and sewer services. It was also expensive to build streets and sidewalks and being close to bus stops and train stations was a necessity. Grocery stores were generally small and located within the neighborhood. Butchers and bakers had their own small shops and milk was delivered to the door by horse drawn carts or motor driven trucks. Schools were located in the neighborhoods and few had playgrounds since there were parks and playgrounds already located in the area.

Entertainment consisted of outdoor sports and activities. Movies were popular and most cities had one or more theaters that hosted films, plays and other traveling shows. Television consisted of a few channels and generally only one television would be in the home. City parks and recreation departments were charged with keeping the park system clean and functional. In the summer, the parks were the babysitters for the neighborhood with paid staff helping children make pot holders and bracelets while older kids played baseball or basketball.

Libraries were a regular stop for many in the community with children checking out the latest books and older gentlemen reading far away newspapers and magazines that were too expensive to have delivered to their homes. Since the libraries were located in the center of town, they were often a beehive of activity and children would often go there to await their parents who worked in a downtown business.

It seems no wonder that cities need to periodically

"reinvent" themselves when conditions warrant. With the advent of the Internet and the proliferation of automobiles, many cities are left scratching their heads as to how to serve this mobile and connected population. Will downtowns ever be busy and relevant again? Will businesses need to have large stores with even larger parking lots when customers can order virtually anything online? Will homeowners ever patronize local theaters and parks when they have a wide variety of entertainment at their fingertips via online delivery services? These are just a few of the topics that will challenge cities for years to come.

Downtowns can play a role in the reinvention of a city but it needs to be done in a way that is consistent with the needs of the community. An evaluation of the existing buildings and an assessment of the accessibility of these buildings can begin the process of reuse and repurposing. Appealing to a multigenerational population is critical to increased foot traffic and business viability. Loft living and unique cafes and stores can appeal to a less vehicle dependent population and provide a lifestyle that is functional and hip.

Fairs and Festivals

"Bluegrass has brought more people together and made more friends than any music in the world. You meet people at festivals and renew acquaintances year after year."
Bill Monroe

What can a city do to attract visitors and create a great quality of life for their residents? Have a fair or festival. A well-planned fair or festival can be a sparkplug to revitalize a community and create a sense of belonging. The type of fair or festival can be as big or as small as a community would like and fit into any budget. In West Virginia, we have fairs and festivals dedicated to "buckwheat pancakes", "strawberries", "apple butter", "Black Heritage", "Italian Heritage" and hundreds of others in every corner of our state. The budgets of these events range from a couple hundred dollars to hundreds of thousands of dollars.

Fairs and Festivals can also be an economic stimulus to an area and create opportunities for small businesses to earn significant dollars. Hotels, food vendors, rental companies and others can increase their business by catering to an area's fairs or festivals. Many cities also plan their events for slow times in order to increase sales for local vendors. Fairs and Festivals can also promote economic development by highlighting a local business or industry. The "Home", "Coal", and "Oil and Gas" festivals provide a way to give exposure to industries while providing people with an enjoyable time.

Maybe the least expensive option for a city is to

organize a fair or festival featuring the city's own departments. I recently attended a 'Fall Festival' in Tega Cay, South Carolina and they invited local non-profits and businesses to participate with the police and fire department at a local park. The turnout was tremendous with thousands of visitors flowing into the park throughout the day. About ten food trucks were in a line dishing out BBQ, Pizzas and deep-fried Oreos. There were large inflatable 'bounce houses' for the kids and a rock-climbing wall for the teenagers. One thing that I really liked was a small, battery powered 'police' car that kids could line up and ride. The police officers helped keep the young drivers on the course and the atmosphere was very positive. It gave the police officers an opportunity to interact with the kids. Likewise, the fire department had a ladder truck on site and allowed the kids to sit in the seat and see what it felt like to drive a fire truck. These interactions are a great way to instill a good image in the children of the community and also may encourage some of them to pursue a career in public safety.

Over the years, I have seen hundreds of interesting fairs and festivals throughout the country. In larger cities, the fairs and festivals are sometimes located in neighborhoods where the streets are blocked off and vendors line the sidewalks. In smaller communities, the fairs and festivals are often promoted with parades featuring bands and floats with 'royalty' of all types. Organizers of these events have learned that involving young people in dance groups and bands tends to attract the parents to the events.

There is really no limit to the creativity that goes into creating a successful fair or festival. Civic clubs, non-profits, youth groups and others are essential along with committed businesses but foremost is the participation of the local "Amazing" City. A city has assets and resources that can make an event successful and provide people and equipment to assist the organizers.

There are few things that have the impact in a city as a successful fair or festival. Creative cities are always on the lookout for new ways to create energy and excitement. A great fair or festival can take a city from great to Amazing!

Food as Economic Development

"Eating is not merely a material pleasure. Eating well gives a spectacular joy to life and contributes immensely to good-will and happy companionship. It is of great importance to the morale."
Elsa Schiaparelli

As I stood in line on Sunday morning buying a half-dozen pepperoni rolls, I thought about how much a particular food becomes associated with the city or region where it originated. The story of the pepperoni roll is well documented in North Central West Virginia. Hundreds of jobs and numerous businesses make a living making and selling these tasty rolls. Cities that take advantage of their association with certain foods can carve out a healthy opportunity for local businesses to increase sales and employment.

One city that does a great job in this regard is Philadelphia, Pennsylvania with its Philly Cheesesteak sandwich. Millions of dollars in sales are racked up each year by mostly small Philadelphia businesses. On a recent trip to Philadelphia, I stopped at a small restaurant and ordered a Philly Cheesesteak. It was unbelievably delicious and was so much better than the 'knockoffs' that I have had outside of Philadelphia. The story of the Philly Cheesesteak is that Pat and Harry Olivieri who owned a hot dog stand near the Italian Market in South Philly invented it around 1930 when

Pat made a chopped steak sandwich on an Italian bun. A cab driver saw Pat eating it and asked him to make him one. After tasting the sandwich, the cab driver told Pat that he should quit making hot dogs and focus on the new "cheesesteak" sandwich. He did, and the rest is history.

Another famous food associated with a city is the famous Chicago 'Deep Dish Pizza'. No trip to Chicago is complete without a slice of the delicious pizza. There are literally hundreds of places to go that range from side-walk food vendors to exquisite restaurants. My favorite is stopping at one of the small Italian pizza parlors that seem to be on every corner and are staffed by friendly Italian proprietors in tomato sauce stained aprons, shouting out your order. With millions of tourists visit-ing Chicago, the small businesses that offer the pizzas gross hundreds of millions of dollars each year.

Seafood dishes are popular in cities like Boston, with its Clam Chowder and Baltimore with its Crab Cakes. These cities have found the benefit of identifying with a popular food and creating the recipes that appeal to a broad segment of the population. It is also important to note that the quality of the food is crucial since many visitors will have had 'versions' of the dishes and expect that the place of origin will be the best of the best.

New Orleans is a city that has made its local food a part of the culture of the city. From Po'boy sand-wiches to the delicious "Beignets" of Café Du Monde, the economy of New Orleans is supported by millions of visitors spending their dollars on foods that are gen-erally unavailable in other parts of the country. When Hurricane Katrina hit the city, one of the things that rallied the citizens was the rich tradition and unique dishes that define the city. Needless to say, the recovery in New Orleans was fueled by the food industry and remains a large economic force.

Many cities could learn valuable lessons in stimulating their economies through the promotion of local food. Local visitor bureaus can assist by maintaining contact information for local food vendors and promoting fairs and festivals. Locally, we see the success of the Blackberry Festival in Nutter Fort, the Strawberry Festival in Buckhannon and the Buckwheat Festival in Kingwood. Thousands of visitors are introduced to these foods and the city becomes associated with these foods in the minds of the visitors.

Just writing this column has me longing for a trip to Memphis to sample a great rack of barbeque ribs or back to San Antonio for a delicious Tex-Mex feast. So until next time, find your favorite Amazing City and sample some of their Amazing foods!

Graffiti—Art or Vandalism?

"Graffiti's always been a temporary art form. You make your mark and then they scrub it off."
Banksy

It is hard to find a city in America that does not have issues with graffiti. As I travel throughout the country, I see graffiti in both large and small cities. Some examples are very colorful and indicate a great degree of style and talent. Others are simply markings on bus stops, benches or other public property. Many cities spend millions of dollars each year removing or repainting graffiti. Businesses also spend money to clean walls and other areas. Movies and popular culture have glamorized graffiti. The availability of spray paint and permanent markers has given the "artists" a quick and effective way to leave their mark on other people's property.

Graffiti has been around for centuries. Examples have been found in ancient Rome and Egypt. The word graffiti comes from the Italian word 'graffito' and is defined as writing or drawings that have been scribbled or scratched on a wall or other surface. I can remember visiting the Pantheon in Rome several years ago and seeing graffiti that had been marked on the stone walls of this building built in 118 AD. Throughout history, graffiti has featured political messages or love poems but seldom has been warmly embraced by city officials or building owners.

On a visit to Poland shortly after the Iron Curtain fell, I remarked to our guide that I could not believe how much graffiti I was seeing on public walls and buildings. He explained that under Communism, young people had no way to express themselves and graffiti was severely punished with jail or beatings. When the wall fell, people went wild with spray paint since it was associated with freedom and the end of communism. Unfortunately, many of the historic buildings are marked with spray paint and give visitors a poor impression of many of these post-Cold War cities.

Many cities have tried alternative methods to deal with graffiti and some are more successful than others. Los Angeles has a program to paint utility boxes along city sidewalks with creative paintings since many of these boxes were frequent targets of graffiti artists. Designating a particular area for 'legal' graffiti has had limited success in some cities and often freeway under-passes, flood walls and parking structures are used to allow people to express themselves in an orderly and legal manner. San Antonio, Texas has developed an underpass art program that has become a popular tour-ist attraction and brings a colorful addition to an area that is generally dull and unexciting.

One challenge to permitting graffiti in cities is the use of graffiti by street gangs. In many large and medium sized cities, gangs have used graffiti to identify "terri-tory" and the police work hard to control this dangerous practice. Some cities prohibit sales of spray paint and markers and many police departments are creating databases of "tags" to identify repeat offenders. Surpris-ingly, very few people actually do graffiti but the ones who do are very prolific and can mark an entire business district in just a night or two.

It is probably impossible to eradicate all graffiti but cities need to develop a multipronged approach to deal with this issue that involves police, community development, youth groups and others. As many have remarked, it is a shame not to harness the talents of these young artists, but to destroy public property in the process it not sustainable. Public art has such a positive benefit. Amazing Cities find creative ways to incorporate "street art" and enhance the culture and character of the city.

Infrastructure

"We need to stop thinking about infrastructure as an economic stimulant and start thinking about it as a strategy. Economic stimulants produce Bridges to Nowhere. Strategic investment in infrastructure produces a foundation for long-term growth."
— Roger McNamee

The crisis in Flint, Michigan is one that may be a warning for the rest of America. We take so much for granted in our country without giving much thought to the aging infrastructure beneath our feet. Roads, bridges, water and sewer lines are aging at an alarming rate and failures have tragic consequences. As I travel around the country, I hear stories of cities that still have wooden sewer lines and water lines that are over one hundred years old.

As our country built its infrastructure over the past two hundred years, having water and sewer service to each and every home was a priority. It signified the prosperity that is such a part of the American dream. Many of us can still remember our parents and grandparents sharing stories of having an outhouse and making that cold journey on a winter night. It seems inconceivable to many people that indoor plumbing is something that was considered a luxury only a few decades ago.

The materials used in getting the water into our homes were often installed with a lack of knowledge as to the health effects of the materials. Lead was used regularly in pipe and the solder used to connect pipes until

1980. Most homes and businesses built before 1980 have lead in their pipes and faucets. Lead was used because it provided some unique properties that prevented pinhole leaks and is soft enough to be formed into shapes that deliver water more efficiently.

The presence of lead in water lines does not necessarily mean that it is dangerous. The chemical reactions of oxygen form a metal oxide layer that protects the water from the lead. Water departments also add lime or orthophosphates to form an additional layer of protection. The water chemistry is something that is vitally important to protect the municipal water supply and points out the need for investment and improvements in technology to protect the water supply. The crisis in Flint, Michigan seems to be due to a failure of the water system to adjust the water chemistry when the supply of water was changed from one supply to another.

Water quality, along with infrastructure is key to our quality of life. When I visited Mexico City several years ago, we were cautioned not to drink the water. Even with the warnings, several people had stomach ailments. Constantly watching to avoid the water had a negative impact on the trip. Even the 2016 Olympics are being impacted by the poor sewage system in Rio de Janeiro in Brazil. The water along the famous beaches is so polluted by the sewage being dumped off shore that officials are worried that swimmers could contract life-threatening diseases simply swimming in the water.

Charleston, West Virginia had a water crisis in 2014 when a chemical leaked into the Elk River and contaminated the water supply for over 300,000 residents. The impact of the water contamination is still being felt. The lawsuits and other litigation have cost several million dollars with more to come. As the crisis with infrastructure spreads across the country, we realize that building an Amazing City requires a constant investment in the systems that give us the quality of life that our citizens expect. Unfortunately, digging up and replacing miles of water and sewer lines does not seem like a great improvement to most taxpayers and the costs escalate each year. The only time that it seems to rise in the public eye is when there is a crisis and then it soon fades from the public eye.

Roads, bridges, water and sewer lines are not the sexy part of government but they are the piece that helps us maintain a unique quality of life. It is expensive and often fails in cities that can least afford the repairs. How we respond to the water issues in Flint, Michigan will give us an indication of the level of commitment our government has to providing everyone with a safe and affordable quality of life.

Another, often unnoticed, infrastructure issue in cities is the 'hidden' walls, sidewalks, streets and other aged assets in our cities. When I was Executive Director of the Sunnyside Up-Campus Neighborhoods Revitalization Corporation we uncovered hundreds of feet of sidewalks, walls and unopened right of ways that added to the walkability and accessibility of the neighborhoods. The value of these overgrown and neglected areas were tens of thousands of dollars and a little tender loving care went a long way in bringing them back to life.

Pittsburgh, Pennsylvania has an unbelievable amount of these hidden treasures and I often like to visit the city to explore this fascinating history. Winding concrete stairways were built in a time when people would sit on their front porches and look out onto the three rivers of Pittsburgh. Spending a little time can restore these magnificent concrete structures and add to the intrinsic beauty of a city.

These are jobs that regular citizens can accomplish and can be celebrated and enjoyed. Boy and Girl Scout troops or other youth groups can participate in these efforts and learn the history of their town by unearthing this historic infrastructure.

My visits to Europe have given me an appreciation for this type of infrastructure and how much it adds to your city. When you see the cobblestone streets in Rome or Budapest, you realize that they have been in place for centuries. A wall along a sidewalk in Brussels is carefully patched when the ground shifts and maintains the historic look. We have adopted a "throw away" mentality in the United States and too often we dig up a hundred feet of sidewalk when a skillful patch would have maintained the walkability for a far smaller investment.

In my experience, we sometimes misread the wishes of the public and take a far too radical approach when dealing with vacant and dilapidated properties. The main objection that most neighbors have to vacant dilapidated properties is the overgrown yards, junk cars and other debris that give the properties an unkempt look. The average cost of demolishing a vacant house can run as high as $30,000 while cleaning up the property and securing the property can be done for as little as $600. Why not clean and secure sixty houses instead of removing one dilapidated structure?

Cities like Detroit, Michigan and Youngstown, Ohio have whole neighborhoods of vacant and dilapidated properties that are hotbeds of drug use and criminal activity. These are tough problems but they are fixable.

With high unemployment and homelessness, programs like those in Albuquerque, New Mexico that employ displaced people to clean up these neglected neighborhoods can have a win-win solution.

Inviting Entrances

"I may or may not be the best fighter in the world but I want to be the best entertainer, so when you see my fights before and after, you'll remember my entrance and the fight. When I've walked in there, you'll know I've walked in there!"
Dave Legeno

Driving down I-77, on a trip to visit my daughter in Lancaster, South Carolina, I saw one of the most beautiful entrances to any city that I have ever visited. A beautifully landscaped knoll with a large brick sculpture welcomed me to the city of Rock Hill, South Carolina. I immediately had a good feeling about this growing Southern town. I had visited Rock Hill several times over the last several years and as I drove into town from several directions, I have observed that the lovely brick entrance signs are a consistent theme at each entrance to the city.

What is the value of a beautiful entrance to a city? I believe that it gives visitors a preview of the city and sets a tone for the visitor or resident. The entrance signage can deliver a subtle message about the city. If it is beautiful and clean, the message can be positive. If it is a worn out sign with overgrown shrubs and grass, the message can give visitors and residents a negative message that is hard to overcome. My own experience, in traveling throughout the country, is that there are few cities that have terrible entrances that then turn out to be Amazing.

The tourism business is very competitive. The

attention to detail of a beautiful entrance can be the difference between success and failure. As my wife and I travel, we often are drawn to a city when we see the entrance sign and are intrigued to visit, often having lunch or dinner and often spending the night. On a recent trip to Key West, Florida, we drove from Miami to Key West passing dozens of small towns along the Florida Keys. As we drove through many of the towns, we saw a variety of entrances and many caused us to stop. Key Largo, Islamorada and Marathon had a welcoming feel and seemed to attract us to stop and enjoy the shops and restaurants. We also entered several towns that had a worn out look to the entrance and seemed to be places that we would rather pass by. For the hundreds of thousands of visitors that drive through the Florida Keys each year, that tattered entrance may be impacting millions of tourist dollars that could otherwise be spent in those communities.

Entrances to cities can also serve to instill a slogan or saying that can help market a city. "The Friendly City", "The Red Rose City", "The Biggest Little City in All the World", and "Racing Capital of the World" are all slogans that entice you to find out more about the city. How many times have you remembered a city because you saw that your favorite actor or hero was born in a particular city? Most times we would have no idea, if this were not noted on the entrance sign to a city. In West Virginia, how many people have learned that Don Knotts was born in Morgantown or that Brad Paisley was born in Glen Dale? Mary Lou Retton's gold medal in the 1984 Olympics literally put Fairmont, West Virginia on the map.

When I speak with city officials, I emphasize that it

is hard to create an Amazing City without having a welcoming entrance. Investing in the entrance to a city can pay huge dividends for a relatively small dollar investment. Even the smallest city can create an appealing entrance with just a little elbow grease and creativity. A nicely landscaped entrance at each entrance to a city can add tremendous value and send a message that the city is truly an Amazing City!

Minor League Baseball: A Success Story

"Love is the most important thing in the world, but baseball is pretty good, too."
—**Yogi Berra**

When city leaders look for ways to build Amazing Cities, more and more are looking at minor league baseball parks as a way to put a spark in the community. As I travel throughout the country, I have visited several minor league parks and watched the economic development that has followed. Big cities have enjoyed major league baseball for decades and it is legend in many large cities. On a recent trip to Chicago, I visited historic Wrigley Field and got to see the impact that major league baseball has in the City of Chicago.

Last summer, I visited Akron, Ohio and visited Canal Park, their downtown baseball park that is home to the Akron Rubber Ducks, a tribute to Akron's history of being the center of the tire and rubber industry. The park seats 7,600 fans and is the place to be on hot summer evenings. Canal Park was opened in 1997 and was constructed by the City of Akron as part of the inducement to obtain the minor league franchise. Akron has done a great job of building downtown housing and developing a good relationship with the University of Akron to encourage a vibrant nightlife in the downtown.

Another outstanding example of minor league baseball as an economic development tool is the beautiful

Bricktown Entertainment District, home to the Oklahoma City Dodgers, a Triple-A team affiliated with the Los Angeles Dodgers. The citizens of Oklahoma City voted for a temporary one-cent sales tax to finance the redevelopment project. The Bricktown development is home to bars, restaurants, theatres and hotels and is a popular place to visit year round. The baseball field is located on Mickey Mantle Drive and features a large statue of the "Mick" at the entrance to the ballpark. The construction cost thirty-four million dollars and seats over 13,000 fans. The park also serves as the field for the Big 12 baseball championships, which draws thousands of fans to the city.

Several years ago, I attended a meeting in Fort Wayne, Indiana and was given a tour of the newly opened Parkview Field by one of the team's owners. The owner, understandably proud, took us throughout the field and showed us the locker rooms, the kitchen, the storage areas and many areas off limits to the regular fans. Seeing thousands of hot dogs being prepared and walking through the money counting room gave us a perspective that few people ever get. The Fort Wayne team is called the Tin Caps after Johnny Appleseed, who serves as the mascot for the team. As evidence of the value of a minor league baseball team to a city, Fort Wayne was named an All-American City in 2009. On August 6, 2009, over 8,500 fans turned out for a game and also to celebrate winning the All-American City designation. The team had over 300,000 fans in attendance for the 2009 season resulting in millions of dollars spent in the city.

Closer to my home, the West Virginia Black Bears of the New York-Penn League, had their inaugural season in the newly constructed Monongalia County Ballpark. The ballpark has led to the construction of a new Interstate exit and millions of dollars of economic development. The ballpark seats 3,500 fans and also serves as the home to the West Virginia University Mountaineer Baseball team. While attendance for the Black Bears has not been released for 2015, the WVU Baseball team averaged over 1,800 fans per game in Big 12 play.

It seems that baseball fans enjoy going out "to the old ballpark" at any level of play. The teams have realized that they are in the entertainment business and feature many other activities to appeal to a wide variety of fans. It is family friendly entertainment and is an economical way to spend an evening. The Fort Wayne ballpark even has a picnic area in the outfield where people can spread out a blanket and watch the game while awaiting a possible homerun ball.

Planning for Reinvention

"The reinvention of daily life means marching off the edge
of our maps."
Bob Black

One of the most important things that a city can do is
to reinvent itself when conditions dictate. A rapidly
growing city may decide that it needs to invest in infrastructure to accommodate the needs of the businesses
and citizens. Likewise, a city that has lost half of its
population because of the loss of a major employer may
need to scale back its budget to avoid a financial crisis.
A city that has primarily been a "bedroom" community
for its larger neighboring city may want to develop a
downtown business district as the population demands.

Over my career, I have experienced reinvention in
many ways. In my first month in office as a councilman in Clarksburg, the city's largest employer, Anchor
Hocking, closed its doors after decades of business. This
required a good deal of readjustment to deal with the
loss of our tax base and the impact on the neighborhoods where most of the employees lived. Shortly after
the plant closure, the devastating flood of 1985 hit us
and impacted dozens of businesses and homes in the
city. The city would never be the same.

As I travel around the country, I visit many cities that
are reinventing themselves. Detroit, Michigan is a good
example of a city in the beginning stages of reinventing themselves. Detroit, which was once a booming city,
has been devastated by the decline of the automobile

industry and a severe population drop. Leaders in Detroit are looking for ways to transform into a viable city once again. It is difficult business. Complete neighborhoods are empty and vacant houses and buildings are plentiful. City leaders have begun to try and revitalize these neighborhoods by inviting artists and others to relocate into houses for the price of one dollar. They are also working to make the downtown safe so that the existing residents and visitors can enjoy the experience. This is tough work and is by no means a guarantee of success.

Other cities that I visit are dealing with other types of issues. In Arizona, the cities around Phoenix are dealing with fast paced growth and an influx of visitors. What were once sleepy, little desert towns have grown into cities of considerable population. Towns that used to barely turn out a hundred people for a high school football game are now hosting the Super Bowl and NASCAR racing events attracting hundreds of thousands of people. This has led to massive increases in city budgets and staffing. Police and fire departments have grown to deal with the influx and facilities to support the residents, like parks and public works have grown substantially. While many people would prefer these types of problems to the issues in Detroit, each can be quite challenging.

How do cities "reinvent" themselves? Proper planning is essential and laying out a plan for the future with citizen involvement is critical to the success of any plan. While it is often time consuming, community meetings, visioning sessions and staff retreats are needed to get ideas from all stakeholders. I also think it is important to bring businesses into the process. They will be important partners and can give needed expertise and guidance. All parties need to understand that their voices are important and that their input will make the reinvention better. Conflict is to be expected. How the city handles the conflict will make for a better outcome.

Reinvention is a huge subject and few cities will survive without some attention to planning for the future. When the process is conducted fairly and with everyone included, a "reinvented city" is an AMAZING City!

Pokémon Go

"Grandpa, is that why you had grandchildren, to help you understand stuff?"
Ali Bartlett

By now you have probably heard about the new phenomena called Pokémon Go. Driving by the Harrison County Courthouse late at night, I saw dozens of young people with their smartphones sitting in small groups and quickly realized that this is something big for cities. How can I be so certain that this is here to stay and not just a passing fad? The reason is that smartphones have been largely a singular activity, keeping teenagers in their rooms or businesspeople sitting quietly by themselves in an airport or restaurant. When the leap is made to bring people together and interact, it is a game changer.

What is Pokémon Go? I will never be considered an expert on this game but I did have a conversation with my granddaughter, Ali and she filled me in on the basics. The game was released on July 6, 2016 and quickly reached record levels of downloads to a wide diversity of players. The technical explanation is that it is a free, location-based, multiplayer game that uses GPS sensors in your smartphone to enable you to travel to things known as "Poke Stops" that are real-life locations in the physical world. The goal is to 'capture' the digital 'insects or critters' and use them in your pursuit of the game.

While Pokémon Go may fade, the idea of using your

smartphone to interact with your fellow residents will grow and develop into valuable business networking and social tools that we can now only imagine. Think about a group of businesses in a downtown, setting up contests or premiums for people who digitally connect and 'collect' a widget when you come in. It is already possible and being developed by the nerds in Silicon Valley and other think tanks, but Pokémon Go took it to the streets with no advertising and relying on word of mouth.

As more and more people of all ages upgrade to sophisticated smartphones, the possibilities will explode. Social outings for senior citizens may become digital history lessons or scavenger hunts that log exercise counts or the like. Business people may hook up in airports or restaurants to collaborate and network between flights or during downtime. Working parents can create carpools and team activities for their children by using the power of the smartphone.

The GPS mapping software app, Waze, is already creating a network of travelers who give up to the minute road conditions and traffic tie-ups. I have used it and found it quickly becomes addictive and a valuable tool for travel, either local or long distance. The future of these types of apps is just beginning to develop. It is not hard to imagine a business that can offer discounts and special deals for travelers in the area. Already, the Waze app alerts me when I am in the vicinity of a Dunkin Donut, a benefit that is adding too many calories, much to my regret.

Cities can really benefit from these types of games and apps since they have a ready-made audience of people who can fill up downtowns and parks for social interaction. There will be some growing pains. Anytime large groups of hormone induced young people get together, the results are sometimes unpredictable, but it does hold tremendous promise. I am sure that the developers of apps and games will come up with a way to bring people together in a safe and productive way.

It is a brave new world with the advent of these digital marvels and I look forward to the Amazing things that will happen in Amazing Cities!

Public Art

"Public art, in all its diversity, can mediate all spaces as Places."
John Newling

I 'm often asked what it takes to be an "Amazing City" and while there are many factors, one that seems to be present in every Amazing City that I visit is a commitment to public art. The *Cloud Gate* sculpture in Chicago is a great example of what I mean by public art. This beautiful, stainless steel sculpture is the centerpiece for Millennium Park and is the subject for hundreds of thousands of pictures each year. Dedicated in 2006, the *Cloud Gate* sculpture draws in visitors from throughout the world and is a favorite of families who park strollers next to the sculpture and let their children find themselves in the reflection of the polished, mirror-like finish.

While many examples of public art are quite expensive, this is not always the case. Public art can be as simple as a mural on the side of a building or a colorful display of a large Adirondack chair in a public square as seen on my recent visit to Albuquerque, New Mexico. Many cities have capitalized on a famous event or person to create a public art display. In Minneapolis, Minnesota, the bronze statue of Mary Tyler Moore throwing her hat in the air is a favorite of many. Nashville and Austin have capitalized on their music heritage and many of the public art pieces reflect a musical theme. In Tulsa, Oklahoma, a large mural of folk hero, Woody Guthrie is very popular and anchors the "Guthrie Green", a large public performance venue.

One Amazing City in Alabama that has put themselves on the map via public art is a small town named Fairhope. I visited Fairhope on a trip to Mobile with the National League of Cities. My good friend, Debbie Quinn was a member of the City Council in Fairhope. She had always bragged about her town being famous for hanging baskets of flowers. I assumed that they had a few flower baskets hanging from the streetlight poles like many cities throughout the country. As we entered Main Street, I was amazed at the hundreds of baskets of beautiful hanging flowers that were everywhere. Buildings, parks, light poles and virtually everywhere else had more flowers that I had ever seen in a city.

The size and scope of public art is as varied as the cities that develop it. Few cities have only one piece of public art. It seems that when cities see the value of developing several pieces of public art, it becomes contagious and everyone starts to think with an "art" mindset. On a recent trip to Los Angeles, I noted the large utility boxes along the sidewalks had been painted with beautiful art. These utility boxes are frequent targets of graffiti and posting of advertising flyers making them very unsightly along the sidewalks. In speaking with some of the Los Angeles city councilpersons, I learned that they have been encouraging putting artwork on the utility boxes as part of neighborhood cleanup efforts.

Public art can also distract focus from objectionable things. In Charleston, West Virginia, a vacant building was an eyesore until a local art group painted plywood panels to cover the broken windows. The paintings made the building appear to have flower boxes and people looking out onto the street. This very inexpensive feature gave new life to the adjoining neighborhood. I have seen this in several cities and it always seems to have a positive impact on the neighborhood.

I am a believer in public art as a component to building an Amazing City. Public art gives a city a fun and lively feel and gives residents and visitors alike, a place to gather. From the largest city to the smallest town, public art is an investment that pays dividends for years and can give your city a needed boost and define your identity.

Public-Private Partnerships

"Corporations often partner with government after natural disasters, as many companies did in the aftermath of Hurricane Katrina in 2005. As a rule, however, long-term civic/corporate partnerships are still rare. But this need not remain the status quo, as many opportunities are available for such partnerships."
Simon Mainwaring

On a trip to the People's Republic of China in 2000, I asked our guide what the words meant on the large globes that lined the downtown sidewalks. She looked at me with a surprised look and said, "Kentucky Fried Chicken, it's from America!" I was somewhat embarrassed, but still found it odd that in a Communist country they had entered into a partnership with a fast food company to provide the lighting along their sidewalks. In countless visits to countries throughout the world, I have found that the United States is somewhat slow to adopt public-private partnerships on a local government level.

Even in Dublin, Ireland, Lord Mayor Christy Burke showed me the Guinness beer taps in his official residence, the Mansion House. They go back hundreds of years and highlight the public-private partnership with one of the city's largest employers, the Guinness Brewery Company. While these might be a little on the unusual side, more and more local governments are seeing the benefit of entering into partnerships that bring value to the city while not increasing the burden on taxpayers.

When I finished my elected career in local government, I was approached by several companies and asked to assist in developing partnerships that met the high test of bringing value to cities while insuring increased value to their citizens. One of the most successful public-private partnerships that I have been involved with has been the National League of Cities Service Line Warranty Program that provides citizens of participating cities with a warranty on their water and sewer service lines and is provided at no cost to the city. The Program is currently being administered by HomeServe USA, an A+ Better Business rated company and continues to save citizens thousands of dollars when they experience a problem with their water or sewer service lines.

Another popular partnership that offers value to many cities is in the energy sector. Large international and national companies have developed very attractive offerings to local governments and school districts around bulk energy acquisition and energy efficiency performance contracting. There are now many smaller companies that are able to bring these innovative partnerships to smaller government units. This promises to grow as more cities realize the benefits. As mentioned in several parts of this book, LED lighting is growing in acceptance and dozens of companies have developed public-private partnerships to provide attractive financing packages for these installations.

Public-private partnerships can sometimes save a needed service during tough budget times and provide a lifesaving service for citizens. An example of this is a program that State Farm Insurance Company offers to states and turnpike authorities. At a time when many Interstate and Turnpike "Courtesy Patrols" are being cut due to tight budgets, State Farm will fund the service in exchange for placing their brand logo on the courtesy patrol vehicles and signage along the highway. This program, which is growing throughout the country, provides a needed service without placing a burden on the taxpayers.

A word of caution on any public-private partnership is to make sure that the companies you are dealing with are at the highest level of ethics and good business practices. Due diligence is essential when vetting possible partnerships. Designing solid requests for proposals where necessary, will avoid problems later on. It is also helpful to look into programs offered by national and state associations like the National League of Cities and the state Municipal Leagues located in each state. A buying service called US Communities regularly saves cities millions of dollars by consolidating purchases with qualified businesses.

I recently had the opportunity to tour the AT&T Stadium in Arlington, Texas and got to see one of the largest and most impressive public-private partnerships in history. Arlington Councilwoman Shari Capehart talked with me during the tour and pointed out that without the support and cooperation of the citizens of Arlington, this "Eighth Wonder of the World" would have never happened. I got to meet the city employee who served as the Clerk of the Works on the stadium project. He spoke with pride about seeing each and every component of the stadium come together. He also said that the most common word that he hears from visitors is,

"That's Amazing!"

The City of San Diego, California has developed an office to coordinate and implement public-private partnerships. They have found that it is beneficial to actively look for ways to partner with businesses in order to bring value to citizens and reduce the burden on taxpayers. Many companies have embraced this concept and work with the city on a regular basis. The office in San Diego is regularly receiving inquiries from other cities to learn about this innovative strategy to work with businesses.

Public-Private Partnerships are here to stay and can provide great value for local governments if properly vetted and managed. Amazing Cities must look for ways to increase value for their citizens if they are to continue to excel and innovate.

Smart City

"Smart cities are those who manage their resources efficiently. Traffic, public services and disaster response should
be operated intelligently in order to minimize costs, reduce
carbon emissions and increase performance."
Eduardo Paes

One of the key trends in local government is the
development of the so-called Smart City movement.
A Smart City is generally defined as a local government
entity that harnesses information and communication
technology to improve the quality of life for its citizens.
As the concept develops, a Smart City may become the
expected level of service in local governments throughout the world. Data is driving many of these initiatives
and the ability of cities to assemble and process data
may be the largest development in local government
in over 100 years. Homeland Security, traffic monitoring, parking enforcement and citizen safety are but a
few of the ways the Smart City can bring value to their
citizens.

With the Internet of Things (IoT) and the development of Google and other commercial online assemblers
of data, local governments have been left to wonder why
they are not at the forefront of this data age. Especially
since they are in a logical position to bring value to their
communities. Progressive city officials are realizing that
if they can harness the volumes of data that are flowing
through their cities, the possibilities are endless.

A pilot program by Uber is being conducted in

Pittsburgh, Pennsylvania to test the acceptability of driverless cars. This program can fundamentally change the way cities look at transportation. It is being driven by data and the presence of Carnegie-Mellon University, located in Pittsburgh, who have led research in this pioneering technology. While there will surely be growing pains as these wheeled robots deal with the hills and climate of the Steel City, there are few obstacles that will stand in the way of this game changing technology.

Infrastructure development and acquisition is another valuable commodity in the growth of Smart Cities. The ability to own and control needed right-of-way will enable cities to gather data and other information that can bring value to citizens. Things like street light and utility poles are a critical link for Smart Cities as they reach virtually every corner of a city and give a convenient access for the installation of monitoring devices, cameras, gunshot locators, Wi-Fi and a plethora of new bells and whistles. A fully integrated, Smart City will make efficient use of space and time to give citizens a level of service that has never before been possible.

To develop a Smart City, city leaders will need to be educated and apply strict protocols in order to maximize return on investment and to make the right choice for the size and needs of the city. In all likelihood, the winners in this movement will be those who understand the technology and educate citizens to avoid misinformation.

Over the past thirty years, technology has transformed what is possible in cities. Development of the Smart City movement is only limited by the imagination of intelligent and resourceful leaders with a vision. What once was a simple process of providing basic services with little more than an adding machine and a billy club, Smart Cities will move forward to revolutionize the lives of citizens and allow for an increased level of safety.

Imagine a city that can send signals via street lighting to alert an active shooter situation or a lost or kidnapped child. Think of smart streetlight fixtures that can sense vibrations or chemical contamination. How about driving directly to an empty parking space in a crowded downtown by a smartphone app? What about a weather warning to residents or targeted descriptions of local sights and amenities? This is only the beginning of an exciting future.

It might seem like a Smart City is synonymous with being an Amazing City but it is important to remember that technology does not take the place of a vibrant, attractive city. Having data that will allow more efficient use of parking and flow of traffic will do nothing for a city if it is dirty and crime ridden. Follow the steps to create an Amazing City and take your city from Smart to AMAZING!

Social Media in Cities

"The PC has improved the world in just about every area you can think of. Amazing developments in communications, collaboration and efficiencies. New kinds of entertainment and social media. Access to information and the ability to give a voice people who would never have been heard."
Bill Gates

You would probably have to be living under a rock not to know that social media has arisen to be a major factor in our cities and how people communicate. Facebook, Twitter, Pinterest and dozens more have invaded our cities and affected how cities operate. As someone who has been involved with city government before social media and after, I can see the good and bad of this new communication tool.

On the positive side, citizens have a way of making their voices heard and providing a sounding board to local officials on issues that affect them. Neighborhood organizations can coordinate activities and grass root groups can do cleanups or neighborhood watch activities in a quick and easy way. Mayors, City Managers and councilmembers can quickly respond to questions or concerns of citizens and get answers to them quicker than newspapers or television.

On the negative side, rumors and nasty remarks can lead to discord within the city. Social media seems to empower people to say things that they would never say in person or even publish in the paper. Neighbors can bicker back and forth and hurtful things can be said that destroys friendships. City officials can get drawn into petty arguments and say things that do not foster cooperation.

I work with city officials throughout the country and I believe that there are some simple principles that can assist cities in using social media without experiencing some of the negative experiences that often happen. The first principle is that social media is a communication tool and should not be used to score political points. Few political arguments are won with a social media post. If city officials are using social media, it should be to disseminate information and not to engage in ongoing discussions.

If someone puts on social media that the city is not plowing the streets after a big snow, it does no good to argue with the person who posted the information. Rather, it is helpful to let citizens know that the trucks are out and that they will be working overtime to complete the job. The message should be positive and not designed to "one up" the original commenter. It takes a thick skin to respond to a post that seems to denigrate the city or its employees but that is what it takes if you are going to respond.

I always adhered to the principle that my response would always be positive, regardless of what the commenter said. It is hard but you would be surprised at the change in attitude when you provide needed information in a helpful manner.

Another important principle is to not discuss individuals in social media posts. In addition to being hurtful, it can also be illegal. Commenting on a police officer's handling of a case can sometimes impact the outcome of a legal case and open the city to liability. If someone has referenced an employee by name, it is helpful to remind the commenter that the city is bound by law not to comment on personnel issues or pending legal cases. Most people know this and will understand the restraint on the part of the city official.

Social media is now a part of city government and using it can bring great benefit to city officials and citizens alike. Following some simple principles can make the experience both informative and enlightening. I believe that we have only scratched the surface on using social media in local government. I am excited to see what is on the horizon. If you would like to see my Facebook page, please visit Amazing Cities with Jim Hunt on Facebook. Feel free to like my page and follow me as I travel the world!

Sports Tourism

"I don't look down on tourism. I live in Hawaii where we have 7 million visitors a year. If they weren't there, there would be no economy. So I understand why a tourist economy is necessary."
Paul Theroux

As I travel throughout the country, a common sight in many cities is a boarded up downtown and dozens of old industrial sites. Graffiti and weeds seem to be taking over and crime is on the rise. The future looks bleak in these cities and their citizens are often discouraged. How does a city recover when the tax base is shrinking and few people want to move to the city?

One city that seems to have found the formula for success is Rock Hill, South Carolina. I recently visited with Doug Echols, the long-time Mayor of Rock Hill and toured some exciting venues that can only be described as "World Class". Doug has seen this once depressed, Southern city experience a rebirth based on sports tourism. Rock Hill had barely 20,000 citizens when Doug decided to enter city government. The once vibrant textile industry was in free fall with most of the manufacturers heading to China to save money. This led to a deterioration of the downtown. Empty buildings seemed to be on every corner.

I asked him how they were able to transform the city into a vibrant city whose population has increased to over 70,000 people with a growing economy. He said that the city leaders realized that in order to turn the city around they would need a solid strategic plan and diversify the economy with a variety of employers. This would keep them from being overly dependent on one employer or industry. The city council and city staff enlisted input from citizens, businesses and others in order to decide the future for the city.

One idea involved building a large athletic complex to attract traveling soccer teams and families who would travel to Rock Hill and spend money with local hotels and restaurants. This started their involvement in the sports tourism industry. It slowly started to show promise. Sports tourism is a great way to spur development but it is very competitive and subject to factors that are often out of the city's control. Many cities have sports venues and host huge events on a regular basis. The Indianapolis 500, the Super Bowl, NFL cities, NASCAR cities and thousands of other events are all part of sports tourism. Participating in this industry often involves maximizing the overall impact of the sport to make it a true contributor to the economy. Hosting a large event once or twice a year might not make a significant impact on a city's economy. In many cases, it might actually cost the city for extra security or traffic control placing a burden on the local budget.

After Rock Hill built their sports complex they decided to focus on bicycle sports and undertook the development of a velodrome. A velodrome is a large structure built of wood or concrete that is used for bicycle racing. There are only a couple dozen velodromes in the United States and few meet Olympic standards. After developing the Giordana Velodrome, Rock Hill decided to expand and develop an entire complex devoted to bicycle sports. Next on the plan was the development of a BMX track.

BMX racing was added to the Olympics in 2008 and is one of the fasted growing sports in the world. Rock Hill's venue has been chosen to host the 2017 World BMX Championship which will attract thousands of visitors from throughout the world. Additional development will include a Criterium track that will also be open to the public for recreational use when not hosting events.

Rock Hill developed these outstanding sports venues without using general fund dollars. They used a combination of hospitality taxes, tax increment financing and public-private partnerships. This creative financing has created additional revenue as more and more visitors stay in local hotels and eat at local restaurants.

There are many other components to the Rock Hill Strategic Plan but sports tourism has contributed greatly to the growth and development of this Amazing City!

The City Sparkplug

"Try to be a rainbow in someone's cloud."
Maya Angelou

Finding the one person who lives and breathes the spirit of a city is like finding gold in a stream. It is rare but valuable, nonetheless. I have been blessed to have worked with several "City Sparkplugs" over my career. My own City Clerk, Annette Wright and Logan, West Virginia's Amber Miller Viars are two who come immediately to mind. They make their cities Amazing by their presence.

When I visited a city in Cuyahoga County, Ohio I walked up to the welcome desk and looked down at the nameplate. It had the lady's name with the title "Manager of First Impressions". I immediately smiled and said that I was going to share this with other cities. She was very personable and directed us to the Mayor's office for our meeting. I am sure many people who are coming to City Hall to complain about one thing or another, change their attitudes completely after meeting the "Manager of First Impressions"!

I have also visited many cities where the person greeting people was anything but nice. It felt like you were bothering them just to ask for directions. Sometimes they would tell you that the Mayor or City Manager wasn't in while I could see the person sitting at their desk through a crack in the door. This type of person gives a very negative impression of the city.

How do you instill a sense of customer service in the

minds of city employees and create several 'city spark-plugs' in the city? It starts by recognizing that everyone has a role in creating a positive image for the city. Office employees, police officers, firefighters, park employees and others can play a valuable role in giving citizens and visitors alike, a great impression of the city. Many cities will hold regular meetings to let employees know that how they interact with the public is a top priority and as important as any other part of their job. When it works, it can change the attitude of the entire city and spread to citizens and others.

Another overlooked opportunity to make a good impression is on the phone. I call many cities in the course of my work. The person answering the phone will often set the tone for my impression of the city. A pleasant voice can send a great message to those people who are calling the city and provide a 'smile' to the person on the other end of the line. Although it is some-times necessary, I think that city government is one of the places that should avoid using voicemail, if at all possible. Imagine a family having a sewer backup and calling city hall, only to get a message saying, "We are currently unable to answer the phone, please leave your name and number." It is not the type of impression that most people would like for their city to deliver.

An Amazing City finds ways to create "sparkplugs" throughout the city and uses every interaction with the public as an opportunity to give a positive impression of the city. Have an Amazing day!

The Power of Parks

"Nature surrounds us, from parks and backyards to streets and alleyways. Next time you go out for a walk, tread gently and remember that we are both inhabitants and stewards of nature in our neighborhoods."
David Suzuki

One of the most important assets in any city is the park system. This has been true for as long as cities have existed. In fact, before the advent of air conditioning and single family homes, parks were a needed part of many cities. Swimming pools, swing sets and ball fields are a treasured memory of countless millions of Americans who grew up considering their neighborhood park as their own front yard. Whether large or small, a park can enhance a city and provide a quality of life for the residents. It is nearly impossible to name a great city, anywhere in the world, that does not have a great public park system.

New York City residents and visitors have enjoyed Central Park since 1857. One of the best known parks in the world, Central Park consists of almost 850 acres and attracts over 40 million visitors each year. It is one of the most filmed places in the world with countless movies and television programs using it as a symbol of New York City. There are thirty-six bridges in the park and several beautiful fountains. Ice skaters can be found throughout the year on the renovated ice rink. Over the years there have been times that Central Park fell into disrepair and it often became the center of political squabbles with politicians running for Mayor and Council pledging to renovate the park.

The Boston Commons in Boston, Massachusetts is another well-known city park and is known as America's oldest park. It sits on 50 acres and connects four neighborhoods in the city. It has hosted numerous concerts and is a popular meeting place for lunch and after work activities. There are several water features in the park with a splash pool and boats shaped like swans that are packed throughout the summer months.

One of my favorite cities which feature great parks is Chicago. The City of Chicago devotes 8.5% of its total land acreage to parkland and is second only to Central Park in New York City with over 20 million visitors each year. Since the 1830's, the official motto of Chicago has been "Urbs in horto", Latin for "City in a garden" for its commitment to green space. It is hard to visit Chicago without being drawn to one or more of its beautiful parks. The parks serve as a gathering place for residents and visitors and also provide miles of bikeways and walkways that are valuable to the physical fitness needs of the citizens.

Amazing parks are not limited to big cities as many of the finest parks are located in smaller communities. I've visited hundreds of cities that have great parks. One in particular is Bluffton, Indiana. I visited Bluffton several years ago and was impressed with their beautiful park system. They have a concert 'clamshell' with acres of green grass and other park amenities. It is located close to restaurants and shopping areas and gives residents a place to spend time with their children in a safe and clean environment.

One thing I have observed is that whether it is a large

or small city, a successful park system has a written plan and which is followed religiously. The plan spells out where they are today and where they intend to be in five or ten years. Good parks take a large investment. It is often impossible to put everything in place in one year, but a plan lets citizens know what is coming and when. The plan allows the local government officials to allocate sufficient funding for needed facilities and maintenance. It also gives local businesses and individuals an idea of possible funding opportunities and ways that they can participate in the park system.

My own life has been positively impacted by the hundreds of hours I spent in city parks learning to swim, playing basketball, and watching my kids and grandkids play t-ball and soccer. An Amazing park system is the sign of an Amazing City. Visit an Amazing park this week!

Part Three

Lessons from Visiting Amazing Cities

The Value of Travel

"Travel is fatal to prejudice, bigotry, and narrow-mind-
edness, and many of our people need it sorely on these
accounts. Broad, wholesome, charitable views of men and
things cannot be acquired by vegetating in one little corner
of the earth all one's lifetime."
Mark Twain

There is no better teacher about local government
than visiting other cities throughout the country
and the world to experience the varied cultures and
traditions that make up our wonderful planet. The following cities are but a few to which I have been blessed
to travel. They have had a great impact on my view of
what makes an Amazing City.

As a young man I feared that I might never travel
outside of the confines of my small town in West Virginia so I jumped at the chance to experience the world
and I have not looked back. As an 8th grader at Central
Junior High School in Clarksburg, West Virginia with
my geography teacher, Mrs. Dodd, I journeyed to New
York City for the princely sum of $58 dollars. I could not
believe the view from the top of the Empire State Building or the destitute men sleeping in the Bowery.

As a senior in college in 1972, I was working for Dr.
Franklin Parker, a Benedum Professor of Education
at West Virginia University, who was an inveterate
traveler. He recommended me to attend the first (and
I think last) Soviet-American Friendship meeting in
Minsk, USSR. Walking in Red Square with St. Basil's

Cathedral in the background and staring at Lenin's Tomb, the world was shrinking and I thirsted for more.

The 7 Keys to Creating an Amazing City have a little of every place that I have visited. In Europe, I have learned an appreciation for history and the need to preserve our past by not tearing down for the sake of the newest "trend". In China, I learned the perils of unrestrained growth and the need for control of the toxic results of a fast moving economy. In Africa, I learned the appreciation for the small steps after years of apartheid and the power of a leader like Nelson Mandela to bring peace to an otherwise violent situation. In Auschwitz, I felt the chill of death in the gas chambers and the need to constantly be on the lookout for man's inhumanity to man.

When I talk to young people I encourage them to travel when they are young so they can use the lessons learned to improve their lives and their communities. I can still remember sitting on the Spanish Steps in Rome, Italy listening to Bruce Springsteen and thinking about the power of public places and how much it means to a city. Years later, our city was going to build another gray, meaningless parking garage and I pushed for something more. We now have a covered structure, reminiscent of the Paris train station, as a multi-purpose structure that, in addition to serving as a parking lot, hosts weddings, festivals and other events.

Travel has given me a more inclusive mind. I find that a lot of my thinking about other races and cultures was formed sitting around tables in Switzerland, Turkey, Korea, Africa and a thousand other places. In Soweto, South Africa, I visited with children who had nothing and asked their teacher if I could donate some money.

The teacher said that I could not donate but the children would be happy to sell us a T-shirt. He said, "We do not want charity, we want opportunity." I can never forget that lesson.

Albuquerque, New Mexico

"When Brian told me he grew up in New Mexico, I told him I thought it is cool that people from other countries play football. He corrected me on my geography and agreed to sit down with me anyway."
Terry Bradshaw

I was excited flying into Albuquerque, New Mexico since it was a state that I had not previously visited. My knowledge of New Mexico was pretty much limited to the large, hot air balloon festival and the fact that the Breaking Bad television program was filmed in Albuquerque. Was I in for a surprise! New Mexico is a stunningly, beautiful state and is filled with many things to do and experience. The area is markedly different from the green hills of West Virginia. It features the desert landscape and adobe construction that we have seen in photographs and art for years. It's called the Land of Enchantment and I can see why.

New Mexico, or *Nuevo México* in Spanish, is often incorrectly believed to have taken its name from the nation of Mexico. However, New Mexico was given its name in 1563, and again in 1581, by Spanish explorers who believed the area contained wealthy Indian cultures similar to those of the Mexica (Aztec) Empire.

Driving around the city of Albuquerque does not give you the feel of a city with over 550,000 residents. It feels spread out. The buildings are fairly small with the largest building in the city being only 22 stories.

We met with several of the city council members and their staffs to present the National League of Cities Service Line Warranty Program. The Service Line Warranty Program is the same one that Shinnston, Bridgeport, Clarksburg and Stonewood adopted to provide protection for their residents from broken water and sewer lines. Not surprisingly, when they learned that I was from West Virginia, they asked about our water problems associated with the tank leak in the Charleston area. Water in New Mexico is a big issue and they have a good deal of discussion about conserving water and protecting it for the precious resource that it is. Unlike a lot of West Virginia, New Mexico cities get most of their water from underground aquifers. If they don't take care of the water, it can impact the aquifer and reduce the quantity. We are somewhat spoiled in West Virginia with our plentiful water supply but we should learn from others that it is necessary to protect water if we expect it to support our residents and businesses.

One program that I was interested in learning more about was Mayor Richard Berry's homeless jobs program. The city has come up with a program that is getting a lot of national attention and involves paying homeless people to work on city streets and parks, cleaning and cutting grass. The program is a great way to provide outreach and interact on a regular basis. It also gives the homeless a hot meal and a way to develop a stable environment. This is the type of win-win program that addresses the issue of homelessness and also provides services to the city that improves the appearance of the city.

I couldn't talk about the great things in New Mexico

without mentioning the great food. New Mexican food is similar to but not quite the same as "Mexican" and "Tex-Mex" foods preferred in Texas and Arizona. New Mexico is the only state with an official question—"Red or green?"—referring to the choice of red or green chili. Combining both red and green chili is often referred to as "Christmas". We found a small restaurant named Cecilia's Café which was listed on the internet as an authentic New Mexican eatery. It was a real treat and as a bonus, the lady who was our waitress was "Cecilia", the owner and namesake of the restaurant.

The staff for the City Council of Albuquerque told us not to leave until we traveled up the Sandia Peak Tramway. The tramway is located at the base of the Sandia Mountains and is quite an experience. The tram holds fifty people and ascends up to around 10,500 feet in only fifteen minutes. There is a restaurant called High Finance at the top of the mountain that offers one of the most beautiful views in New Mexico. As you look over the entire city, the setting sun and the lights are fantastic. The tram is similar to the New River Gorge Bridge in West Virginia in that it attracts tourists to the area and serves as a great economic development tool and job creator.

We drove down to Santa Fe, the state capitol of New Mexico and spent the night in the Hotel Santa Fe, a Native American owned hotel located in the downtown area. I stopped by the New Mexico Municipal League and spoke to Bill Fulginiti, the Executive Director, about issues that were affecting New Mexico cities. I have known Bill for several years and he loves his adopted state of New Mexico. He said that New Mexico cities are fighting to keep the state legislature from negatively impacting the budgets of cities. I shared with him that this is pretty much a common theme in most of the states I visit including West Virginia.

The league's offices are located right across the street from the State Capital which is an unusual looking building for someone familiar with our beautiful capitol building in Charleston. The New Mexico capitol building is unique in that it is the only round capitol building in the United States. While standing in front of the building, I heard someone say, "Hey, Jim." I couldn't figure out who would know me in New Mexico and as I turned around, I saw the staff members that we met with in Albuquerque the day before. They were impressed that I took the time to visit their State Capital.

Although I only spent two days in New Mexico, I realized that it was a place that would be worthy of a return trip. Much like West Virginia, the people were friendly and went out of their way to be helpful.

Amsterdam, Netherlands

"Amsterdam was a great surprise to me. I had always thought of Venice as the city of canals; it had never entered my mind that I should find similar conditions in a Dutch town."
James Weldon Johnson

In everyone's life, they should try and visit Amsterdam just once. I was fortunate to travel to The Hague in the Netherlands, to attend the 1st City Diplomacy Conference in 2008 and took time out for a visit to Amsterdam. It was a fairly short train ride from The Hague and I arrived at the train station in Amsterdam to see one of the most amazing sights that I have ever encountered. Bicycles! Yes, thousands of bicycles were parked in massive rows surrounding the train station. It seemed as if everyone rode bicycles. You would see families, business people, and girls in fine dresses riding along the streets of the city. It was hard to imagine how people would find their bike amid this sea of bicycles but I'm sure they have a system.

Occasionally you would see a lone bike hanging from a tree or a bridge that was abandoned or dumped there by a bicycle thief.

It is easy to get around in Amsterdam and no matter which direction you head you see some interesting sights. The bridges throughout the city seem to be on every corner, along with interesting houseboats on the canals that traverse the city. Public art is everywhere. The benches that were covered in colorful ceramic tiles particularly impressed me. There was also an interesting group of people that you encountered on the streets. Street performers, hippies, homeless were but a few of the groups that were throughout the city. You would go from a guy juggling knives to a mime working the crowd. Amsterdam also attracts a lot of people from throughout the world because of its 'anything goes' attitude. Marijuana is legal and the pot bars are on many corners. In some outdoor cafes, the smoke is heavy and people are lounging on couches and chairs throughout.

Prostitution is also legal and there are "window girls" in many shops interspersed with cafes and bars. It is an unusual sight to be walking down a street, looking in a store window and seeing a scantily clad lady looking back at you. I read that this is a tradition that goes back centuries that the government is trying to eliminate or reduce.

Needless to say, I have never seen such a thing in my many travels.

The multistoried houses that line the narrow streets are also interesting as all of them have a large hook in the peak of the house. I was told that these were 'furniture' hoists to allow people to get furniture and other large items to the upper floors since the houses had narrow stairways. The houses were very colorful with an interesting mix of pastel colors and all of them having flower boxes on every level. I can assure you that I will not forget the beauty of the streets with the aroma of flowers and the beauty of the houses.

Another sight that is quite common is the orange color of the national football (soccer) team. I was there during the World Cup and it seemed that every other bar had orange flags, banners and the like throughout the building. One bar was completely painted in orange and the crowd was stuffed into the building drinking beer and cheering at every play.

While Amsterdam might not be on everyone's wish list, it is an eclectic city with a vibe unlike anywhere in the world. The scenery is beautiful and the people were friendly and welcoming.

Auschwitz, Poland

"Sometimes I am asked if I know 'the response to Auschwitz; I answer that not only do I not know it, but that I don't even know if a tragedy of this magnitude has a response."
Elie Wiesel

As the first week ended on the Habitat for Humanity build in Wroclaw, Poland, we embarked on a day trip to visit the Auschwitz Concentration Camp, which was about two hours from Wroclaw. The drive was pleasant as we traveled through the countryside and saw the well-kept farms and fields of corn and other crops. As we approached the former concentration camp, I was stunned to see how close it was to the farms and villages. I had always thought that these camps were located far from civilization and that was the reason they could be operated with impunity. It was shocking to realize that they were out in the open and many chose to ignore the atrocities that were occurring within.

Walking into the camp you are met with the infamous motto, "Arbeit macht frei" (Work brings freedom) spelled out in wrought iron above the gate. It is an imposing site and one that still brings an emotional feeling. There is an eerie silence as you enter, as if you are visiting a shrine or cemetery. A young girl of about 20, who would be our guide, met us. She walked us through the main buildings where the staff were housed and pointed out the desks and file cabinets that have been reconstructed as part of the museum. We next visited the barracks where the prisoners were held. The wooden bunks were crammed into the drafty wooden buildings and our guide explained that there would be hundreds of prisoners in buildings that were designed for twenty or thirty. The bathrooms consisted of long wooden troughs that the prisoners would have to empty by shoveling waste into buckets. Our guide explained that thousands of prisoners died of disease and starvation. It is estimated that over 1.1 million people were killed during its operation.

As we made our way to the gas chambers, I was not prepared for the life changing feelings that would hit me. Our guide directed us into a small block building, she pointed out the piping coming out of the ceiling. She explained that the prisoners were told that these were the showers that were needed before that boarded trains out of the camp. When hundreds were stuffed into the room, the cyanide-based gas called Zyklon B was pumped into the room through the piping. Standing in the room, you could literally feel the souls that had perished there. As the gas quickly killed the prisoners, they were then carted off to the crematorium for incineration. It was explained that so many bodies had been burned that disposal of the ashes became a problem and they spread many of the ashes on the farmland near the camp.

We finished our tour near the wall where many prisoners were shot and the markings of thousands of bullets were still visible. As our guide finished her remarks she told us that each year there are fewer and fewer visitors to the former concentration camps as the events of World War II seem a distant memory to many. As she spoke, she started to weep. She said that working as a guide, she meets so many who had relatives who died in the camp that it is impossible not to be affected by the growing complacency of those who do not remember the horror of World War II.

I will never forget my visit to Auschwitz and the impact that it had on my life. The events can never be described in words or displays. I had visited the Holocaust Museum in Washington, DC and watched the movie, Schindler's List, but nothing can duplicate the utter horror of this place. I would encourage people to study the Holocaust and keep the memory alive of the millions of Jews, homosexuals, Gypsies and others who were exterminated by the Nazis. God rest their souls.

Austin, Texas

"People don't live in Austin to work; they work to live there."
Robert Rodriguez

It doesn't take long to realize that Austin, Texas is a place where live music is played and appreciated. Stepping off of the plane you are greeted by the sound of live music being played at the Austin City Limit store. It is also easy to know you are in Texas with cowboy hats and boots on many of the travelers who are walking in the airport.

On the cab ride to the hotel we passed some longhorn cattle in a field and they are truly an amazing sight. The horns are easily six feet across and you can see why they are used as the symbol for many things in Texas.

Austin is growing and there are new buildings going up throughout the city. Seeing dozens of construction cranes against the skyline is indicative of the rapid growth. Austin's population is over 885,000 residents and shows no sign of slowing down.

Austin is also home to the University of Texas and the campus is close to the downtown. The Darrell K. Royal football stadium is a prominent structure on campus and holds over 100,000 fans. I was interested to learn that the Texas-WVU game on October 6, 2012 holds the record for attendance with 101,851.

The LBJ Library is also on the campus of the University of Texas and is one of the most interesting museums that I have ever visited. The building holds over forty-five million pieces of paper, contained in red boxes that occupy four floors of the building. There is also a replica of the Oval Office and Lady Bird Johnson's office. Each floor of the library has several phones on which you can listen to President Johnson talk to leaders and others. You could easily spend several weeks learning about President Johnson and the significant events of the sixties.

The most unique feature of the library was a life size, animatronic robot of President Johnson, telling humorous stories. This was so well done that after a few minutes, it felt like the President was speaking to you.

Austin attracts a wide variety of people and a favorite saying is "Keep Austin Weird". The city is truly Amazing and I look forward to visiting again in the near future.

Belfast, Northern Ireland

"I certainly notice the vitality in Belfast, which wasn't there in the Seventies. There was a war going on then. Now there are cranes everywhere. There really is a sense of renewal and hope."
Liam Neeson

When I told people that my wife and I were going to visit Northern Ireland, many people asked if it was safe. The violent history in Northern Ireland would lead you to believe that this might not be the case. Random terrorist attacks, as recent as last year, would not encourage many visitors to make this a stop on a visit to Ireland. I did some research and learned that Belfast in Northern Ireland has become a safer city and is overcoming its violent past. I was still a little concerned but booked a train ticket from Dublin and scheduled a meeting with a member of the Lord Mayors Planning staff to discuss how a city deals with the overwhelming challenges of terrorism and violence.

The train ride to Belfast is a beautiful experience. The green Irish countryside passes by the window of the train like a movie. Cows and sheep graze on small farms with little cottages and seemingly endless stonewalls. Arriving at the Belfast Central Train station is like going back in time with an old brick building, overgrown grass and litter blowing in the cold wind. A taxicab pulled up and I started to rethink my idea of visiting this historic city. We went into our hotel and learned that the rooms would not be ready for a couple of hours. We decided to take a walk around the city and see if we could find a nice restaurant for lunch. As we walked, it appeared that our selection of restaurants was pretty slim. We headed down a dark street to a familiar Subway sign. After a six-inch sub and a Diet Coke, we thought it best to head back to our room and bolt the door.

Surprisingly, as we walked to the end of the street, we were surprised to see a town square with a flurry of activity and dozens of fashionable stores in an area called Victoria Square. There were families with young children and couples enjoying the day. At a large sculpture in the center of the square were three young men doing a street dancing performance with a large crowd surrounding them. It was so impressive our minds were immediately changed about the city. As we walked back to the hotel, we saw the beautiful City Hall where our meeting was scheduled for the next morning.

The Belfast City Hall is one of the most beautiful city halls in the world. It was built in 1906, when Belfast was a thriving city with shipbuilding, rope manufacturing and linen production making it one of Europe's most prosperous cities. The building takes up an entire city block. There are numerous statues and gardens within the tall iron fence that surrounds the property. Of particular interest is the Titanic Memorial that honors the many Belfast residents who lost their lives when the ship encountered an iceberg on its maiden voyage. The Titanic was built in the Belfast shipyards. Its crew and many passengers came from the city. The memorial consists of a large statue with a bronze plaque listing all of those who lost their lives when the ship sank.

My meeting with Sharon McNicholl, the director of planning and policy development for the Belfast City

Council was very interesting. She provided an overview of how Belfast has come back from its troubled past. One key that she mentioned was the focus on the city center and making sure that people had an attractive place to visit and spend time. After about an hour, our meeting concluded and we were given a private tour of the Belfast City Hall. We went into the City Council chamber and they let me sit in the Lord Mayor's chair, which was a thrill.

As we left the Belfast City Hall, I was moved by the dedication and commitment on the part of the city officials. They have put together a plan to improve the quality of life for the citizens and build a thriving tourist industry.

Northern Ireland has been in conflict for much of my adult life in a time described as the "Troubles". It is the conflict between the Catholics and the Protestants. It has cost many lives and devastated the economy of Northern Ireland. Between 1969 and 1998, much of Northern Ireland was at war with British troops fighting the IRA and neighborhoods divided between Catholics and Protestants. In 1998, President Bill Clinton negotiated a peace settlement and sent former Senator George Mitchell to work with both sides on a path forward. Belfast was at the center of much of the violence and suffered during this period. Although there are still many issues that divide the city, they have made remarkable progress in rebuilding the city center and bringing life back into the city.

In order to see the extent of the division, we booked, what is called a "black cab tour" of many of the trouble spots. The driver was named "Paddy". He picked us up at our hotel and gave us a briefing on what we would be seeing. He explained that he lost three family members during the conflict and had moved to England to avoid the violence and raise his family. He moved back to Belfast as the conflict was winding down and began driving a cab, giving tours of the trouble spots to those brave enough to go. As we drove into the Catholic side of Belfast, he pulled up to a metal wall and parked the cab. My wife looked at me and I have to admit to being a little scared. He jumped into the back seat and told of the beatings and murders that took place on that street. He told us how his wife would worry if one of their five sons were even a few minutes late in coming home.

We then drove to Fall's Road which was lined with large murals describing the conflict and pictures of those who lost their lives. It was a sobering experience. The light rain and overcast skies made it even more so. Murals have been used for years to document the struggle in Northern Ireland. It is estimated there are over 300 murals in Belfast alone. We then stopped at the headquarters of Sinn Fein, the political party that was thought to be associated with the IRA during the conflict. The building has a large mural of a young poet and member of the British Parliament named Bobby Sands who died after a hunger strike in prison in 1981 at the age of 27.

There were plaques and memorials on the Sinn Fein building and you could sense it was at the center of the neighborhood. Interestingly, Britain's Prince Charles visited Ireland during our time in the country and shook hands with Gerry Adams, the head of Sinn Fein in what was thought to be a move forward in the peace process. Prince Charles lost his great-uncle, Lord Mountbatten in an IRA bombing in 1979.

As we entered the Protestant section of Belfast, Paddy explained that at 6:00 p.m. each day, the gates are closed in both the Catholic and Protestant neighborhoods until 6:00 a.m. to keep the threat of terrorism down. This was astonishing to me, to think that this is a way of life for these citizens. The wall, with a metal fence reaches over thirty feet and houses along the wall have heavy metal screens installed to prevent rocks and firebombs from being hurled over the wall. We finished our tour and bid our driver, Paddy, a warm goodbye. He left us with his thought that the wall will come down in his lifetime. He said that most people do not share his optimism but that he sees small but significant changes. I hope he is right and that Northern Ireland will find a lasting peace.

Brussels, Belgium

"In Brussels, you are able to have a lot of appointments in a day. In Paris, you can have one, two, maybe three, but you spend all your time on the road, in the car or in the suburbs. In Brussels, everything is easy. It's not a very big city, and the people are very quiet and warm."
Eric-Emmanuel Schmitt

In 2005, I was selected, along with twelve other rural government officials, to participate in a fellowship to study rural development issues in Europe. The fellowship was hosted by the European Union, which is located in Brussels, Belgium. Brussels is a city of over 1.8 million residents and since the end of World War II is a major center for international politics. I had never visited Brussels and I was excited to share the experience with my wife Pam, on her first trip overseas. She was a little reluctant to venture out on her own but she slowly got used to the new environment.

Our hotel was in the city center and the rooms were somewhat small, but comfortable. The breakfast buffet was worth the trip and featured an array of pastries and fruits that got us started on the busy schedule. My meetings took up most of the mornings and early afternoon but there was plenty of time to explore this beautiful city. It is centuries old and the cobblestone streets and small shops are a visitor's delight.

Brussels is home to a diverse mixture of architecture spanning from the medieval buildings on the Grand Place to the postmodern buildings of the European

Union. The main attractions include the Grand Place, a UNESCO World Heritage Site, the Gothic Town Hall and the Royal Palace of Laeken with its large greenhouses. We visited the famous fountain of the little boy urinating called *The Manneken Pis* and stood in line for a picture. The fountain is a favorite tourist attraction and symbol of the city.

Another unique structure is the Atomium, a 338 foot tall structure composed of nine steel spheres connected by tubes which forms a model of an iron crystal. It was built for the 1958 World's Fair and is a memorable site.

A highlight of the trip was a visit to the small town of Bruges, one of the most picturesque places in Europe. Bruges looks as though time had stopped in the 1800's. Canals wind their way through the historic buildings with the occasional swan basking in the sunlight. The flowers were beautiful and the whole city looked like a beautiful fairy tale. It is called the "Venice of the North". The town square was the perfect setting for our evening meal in an outdoor restaurant.

The cuisine in Belgium is a combination of French and Flemish. The Belgium waffles are world famous and start the day out right. There are over 1800 restaurants in the city. It is considered among connoisseurs as one of the best cuisines in Europe. We especially enjoyed the small cafes that had one or two tables in front. My wife and I would sit for hours with our favorite Belgium beer and watch the people walk through the city.

The pace of life seemed to be a step or two slower than what we were used to and that was kind of nice. I can hardly imagine a better place to escape the worries of the day than Brussels.

Caux, Switzerland

"Switzerland is a small, steep country, much more up and down than sideways, and is all stuck over with large brown hotels built on the cuckoo clock style of architecture."
Ernest Hemingway

In 2002, Pastor David Kates and I were invited to present a program at the Connecting Communities Conference held in Caux, Switzerland. We had been working on The Unity Project in Clarksburg and it attracted the attention of Rob Corcoran from a group called Initiatives of Change in Richmond, Virginia.

Rob has worked throughout the world and was interested in how a small city like Clarksburg was able to react so positively to an announced visit of the Ku Klux Klan to Clarksburg.

While we were honored to be invited, we didn't know how we would be able to afford to travel such a long distance. Fortunately, Pastor Kates had received an award from the National Black Mayor's Association, which included a cash award, and with the help of a few other supporters, we decided to attempt the journey. Pastor Kates had never been overseas and needed to get a passport along with a new set of luggage.

I should also mention that Pastor Kates was terrified of escalators. We had to plan our trip with the knowledge that we would avoid all escalators from Clarksburg to Switzerland. We flew out of Pittsburgh via London and on to Geneva, Switzerland, all without using an escalator. When we would get on the elevator, we would be surprised when almost everyone on it would say that they too had a fear of escalators.

When we arrived in Montreux at the base of the Alps, we saw the sign for Caux. It was located up in the Alps and we needed to get on a small train that climbed the mountain with a cogwheel propelled by the engine. The luggage was loaded on a wagon that was pushed in front of the train. We climbed up the mountain and stopped at several small villages on our way to Caux. When we arrived at Caux, it was high above the clouds and we were looking down on small airplanes and gliders circling above Lake Geneva.

Caux is a small village of about one thousand residents and a large hotel/conference center that was donated to the Initiatives of Change organization after World War II. Its purpose was to bring people of all backgrounds from throughout the world to address issues of peace and understanding.

As we checked in, we were assigned our rooms and saw a diverse group of people standing in line and milling around the lobby. We unpacked and made our way down for our orientation session at the conference. It was then that Pastor Kates asked me where the television was in the room. I told him that they didn't have them and he said that was a problem, as he needed it to fall asleep at night. It was only his first surprise of the trip!

During the orientation, we were informed that each conference participant would take their turn working in the kitchen, serving meals or doing dishes. This was explained as a way to involve everyone in the work and bring people together.

They told us that Prime Ministers, Members of

Parliament and others had all done this over the many years of the center. Pastor Kates shot a look at me from across the room, wondering what I had gotten him into.

The participants in the conference came from throughout the world. Russia, Ukraine, Moldova, Israel, Iran, South Africa, Italy, Scotland, Ireland and dozens of other countries were all present. We quickly made friends. The work in the kitchen was a good way to meet and talk to people as you cleaned plates and washed dishes adorned in burgundy aprons. Pastor Kates was quickly a favorite and many people wanted to meet this fellow from America.

The sessions were very interesting and discussions went well into the evening. There were both young and old, with some talented musicians who would play guitar and share songs from their respective countries. A little fellow from Australia named Johnny Huckle was a crowd favorite as he sang a wide variety of songs and kept us entertained for hours. As always, when he played "Country Roads", everyone joined in and we proudly sang along as the only West Virginian's in the house.

Our presentation was going to be translated into five languages. We were reminded to speak slowly as the interpreters needed time to do their work. When we told the story of the Ku Klux Klan coming to Clarksburg, every eye in the room was on us. Pastor Kates did a great job of speaking and mesmerized the audience.

At the conclusion of our session, dozens of people came up and continued to ask about our little town in West Virginia. We also took the time to present a group of kids from Moldova with the Key to the City of Clarksburg. We didn't tell them we were going to do it and they were so surprised that they started to cry. We also passed out T-shirts from the Clarksburg Fire Department and many of the young people wore them each day.

The trip was so enjoyable and I was pleased to take Pastor Kates on his only overseas trip. He passed away a few years later. I will never forget this giant of a man. He is missed in Clarksburg and around the world as he made an impression on these young people as a man of peace.

Charleston, West Virginia

"In West Virginia yesterday, a man was arrested for stealing several blow-up dolls. Reportedly, police didn't have any trouble catching the man because he was completely out of breath."
Conan O'Brien

It would be hard to count the number of times I have traveled down Interstate 79 to visit our state capital, Charleston, West Virginia. It is often easy to take it for granted, but Charleston is one of the unique cities in America. The Capitol Building, sitting on the banks of the Kanawha River is one of the most majestic seats of government in the United States. The blue and gold dome atop the capitol building creates a backdrop that signals dignity and respect. Noted architect, Cass Gilbert, designed the building and was so pleased with the final product that he used parts of the design when he designed his final work, the United States Supreme Court Building in Washington, DC.

The downtown business district of Charleston is typical of large, American cities and features many unique buildings and an attractive streetscape. Charleston is similar to Pittsburgh, in that rivers and hills dominate the city with few residents living in the downtown district. Bridges also dominate the city. When the Interstate Highway System was developed, they chose to cut a swath through the city and changed many of the historic neighborhoods.

Charleston features one of the most successful Urban Redevelopment Projects in the country. The Charleston Town Center is a downtown mall which was opened in 1983 and is the largest downtown based mall east of the Mississippi. The Town Center is a popular place for visitors to Charleston. During events in the city, the mall becomes a popular meeting place for attendees. There are several hotels and the Charleston Civic Center in the area around the Town Center. The city regularly hosts statewide events and concerts that are a big part of the economy of the city.

One of the most impressive events in Charleston happens every four years with the inauguration of the governor. I have been honored to attend several inaugurals and each has been a memorable occasion. Charleston rolls out the red carpet and is alive with activity during the inaugurals. Parties, concerts and the ceremony in front of the capitol rank as highlights in my many visits to Charleston.

Another stop that is sure to be enjoyable to any West Virginian is the West Virginia Cultural Center. While I had visited the Cultural Center for many performances of the popular live radio program, Mountain Stage, I had never visited the exhibits until I attended a conference of the West Virginia Municipal League last year. It is a living, visual history of West Virginia. I cannot imagine anyone who would not enjoy the tour. One exhibit that connects with Central West Virginia is the library room of the Goff House that was located next to the Central Fire Station in Clarksburg. It is a beautiful example of a bygone time and an integral part of the history of Clarksburg and the State of West Virginia.

So if you are looking for an exciting weekend or a fun filled day trip, Charleston, West Virginia offers a lot of possibilities and is just two hours down the highway. Take the kids and walk up the steps to the capitol and walk around the grounds. It will give you a new perspective and make you proud to be a West Virginian. Safe travels.

Chicago, Illinois

"Eventually, I think Chicago will be the most beautiful great city left in the world."
Frank Lloyd Wright

A couple of weeks ago, I had the opportunity to, once again, visit the beautiful city of Chicago, Illinois to meet with my longtime friend, Joe Moore. Joe is an Alderman in the 49th Ward who has served in office since 1991. I first met Joe on a National League of Cities trip to the People's Republic of China in 2002 and we have kept in touch ever since. There are fifty wards in the City of Chicago and each has an elected Alderman to represent its citizens. Chicago has over 2.7 million citizens, which makes it the third largest city in the United States.

After a quick flight from Pittsburgh, I landed at O'Hare International Airport and jumped in a cab for the trip to the hotel. The cab ride can take from one to two hours depending on the traffic. Luckily, traffic was not bad and we made it to the hotel in about an hour and five minutes. The hotel was called the Buckingham Athletic Club and Hotel. It is located close to the Chicago City Hall on LaSalle Avenue.

When I went into the building at 440 LaSalle Avenue, it looked like a typical office building, with no sign of a hotel desk clerk. I approached the small desk in the center of the lobby and asked the lady where the hotel was located. She said, "You're here." She explained that the hotel is located on one floor of the office building and was unlike most hotels around. I got on the elevator and sure enough, you get off on the 39th floor to transfer to a private elevator to go to the 40th floor. Probably one of the strangest hotel arrangements I have ever seen!

Chicago has a unique look and feel with the elevated train tracks going throughout much of the downtown. You might remember the opening of the *Bob Newhart Show* was set in Chicago and showed the elevated trains and multiple bridges in the downtown area. As we made our way to the Chicago City Hall, I was looking to see if Dr. Robert Hartley (Bob Newhart) or his wife Emily (Suzanne Pleshette) were taking a quick lunch at one of the famous deep-dish pizzerias.

The Chicago City Hall is located on LaSalle Avenue and was dedicated in 1911. My colleague, Brian Davis and I met Alderman Moore in his office. After our meeting, he gave us a tour of the Council Chambers. The City Council Chambers has seats for each of the fifty aldermen and reminded me of the Belfast City Council Chambers I had visited in May. The City Hall also has a "green" roof that was completed in 2001 and has over 38,800 square feet of roof gardens. The garden consists of over 20,000 plants with more than 150 species, including vines, shrubs and two trees. The green roof design was done to serve as a pilot project to encourage other buildings to adopt green building practices.

As we were getting ready to leave City Hall and bid Alderman Moore goodbye, he was notified that a meeting he had scheduled for that evening had been canceled. "How would you like to go with me to the Chicago Cubs game at Wrigley Field tonight?" he asked. Wow, what could be more Chicago than attending a Cubs game at Wrigley Field?

While I am not the biggest baseball fan, a chance to attend a game at Wrigley Field to see the Cubs play the Los Angeles Dodgers was something I could not pass up. Wrigley Field is one of the most iconic baseball parks in America and takes you back to a time long ago. Wrigley Field opened in 1914 and is known for the ivy-covered walls in the outfield and the unusual wind patterns coming off of Lake Michigan. It is also unique for being the last major league baseball park to have lights installed in 1988.

Our host, Alderman Joe Moore met us at a small restaurant near Wrigley Field where we dined on fish and chips along with several beers before going to the ballpark. The experience of going to a baseball game in Chicago is unique with thousands of fans roaming the neighborhoods surrounding the field creating an electric feeling in the air. It seems as though everyone is wearing a baseball shirt with his or her favorite player's name on the back.

We walked through the turnstiles and headed to our seats. I was expecting to be far away from the field and was pleasantly surprised when Alderman Moore led us to our seats about six rows behind home plate. He explained that he has had the seats for several years and would attend the games with his sons until they grew up and moved to college. It was nice attending the game with the Alderman, as he seemed to know most of the people in the park. The beer vendor came over to greet us and told us that he and Joe have been friends for many years.

Sitting behind home plate affords you a tremendous view of the game and also lets you see the many buildings surrounding the field that have bleachers installed on their roofs for the fans. Joe told us that this was a great tradition when people would set lawn chairs on the roofs and watch the games. Over the years, the value of the buildings increased and the owners began to sell tickets and refreshments to the fans. A controversy occurred over the past several years when the current owners of the Cubs constructed a new, electronic scoreboard that blocked the view of many of these "unofficial" outfield seats.

The game with the Dodgers was exciting with several home runs and lots of action. There was also a unique weather event during the game when a blanket of clouds, called Mammatus clouds, filled the sky and made for a beautiful backdrop for the historic field. We didn't learn till the next morning that several tornados had touched down south of the city.

Seeing the Cubs win at Wrigley Field was an unforgettable experience and having such a great host, as Joe Moore made this trip to Chicago, one of my favorites.

Cleveland, Ohio

"My mom bought me a white Strat, but that wasn't what I wanted, so I went to a guitar store in Cleveland and - the guy told me it was a really good deal - made an even swap for a blue Teisco Del Ray. I loved that guitar and used it a bunch."
Dan Auerbach

Remember the Drew Carey Show and the anthem to Cleveland called Cleveland Rocks? Growing up I would hear stories about Cleveland and see stories about the Cuyahoga River catching on fire from all of the pollution in the river. Over the years I had several visits to Cleveland that seemed to contradict the stories that were written about Cleveland. I attended the CART Indy races that were held on the Burke Lakefront Airport, on the shore of Lake Erie. Seeing Mario Andretti and Paul Newman walking around the pits was a thrill and delicious dinners in the former warehouse district called "The Flats" were memorable.

I spoke at a meeting of the National Black Caucus of Local Elected Officials in 2006 and received a warm welcome. I also got to visit the Rock and Roll Hall of Fame. The Rock and Roll Hall of Fame is a real treat. The exhibits are interesting and celebrate the music and artists my generation grew up on. So I had a pretty positive view of Cleveland and enjoyed any opportunity to visit the area.

My recent visits to the area have only reinforced my feelings about Cleveland and Cuyahoga County. As the most populous county in Ohio, Cuyahoga County is home to 57 cities and over 1.2 million citizens. The county has a wide diversity of living arrangements which goes from urban living to rural villages with open spaces. Each of the cities in the county has some unique features that make them nice places to live. When many of the cities were founded, they dedicated large areas for city facilities and parks. It is not unusual to see the city hall, library, swimming pool, baseball fields and senior center located together which makes for a nice arrangement. This type of city planning provides a very nice quality of life and gives citizens a meeting place that is not associated with shopping areas.

On one of my visits to Cuyahoga County, we went to the Bedford Heights City Hall to meet with the Mayor and President of the City Council. Bedford Heights is a city of 10,700 residents and is adjacent to the city of Bedford. The Mayor is Fletcher Berger and the President of the City Council is Phil Saunders. Mr. Saunders should be familiar to many people in Harrison County as he is the son of E.B. Saunders, the longtime principal of Kelly Miller School which was located on Water Street in Clarksburg. E.B. Saunders was a prominent figure in Clarksburg and was honored by the Clarksburg City Council several years ago by renaming Water Street to E.B. Saunders Way. I have met Phil Saunders on many occasions at National League of Cities conferences and it was an honor to see him in his hometown where he has created his own legacy of leadership and community service. Phil was just one of many West Virginia residents who migrated to the Akron-Cleveland area to pursue jobs in the rubber and steel industries.

One thing that sticks out from visiting with city

officials in Cuyahoga County is the many services that they provide for their citizens. On one occasion, I observed a gentleman leaving City Hall with a chain saw. I mentioned to the Mayor that it was an unusual sight coming out of city hall. The Mayor explained that the city has several pieces of equipment that residents can check out, much like a library. It is a well-received service since many of the items are things that you might only need for a few hours during the year. I was also surprised to find out that many cities in Cuyahoga County provide residents with lawn cutting, snow removal and other services. This was somewhat shocking and something I had never imagined we could afford during my City Council career in Clarksburg. I asked these officials how they could afford to provide this level of service for their citizens. Alas, they were struggling with their budgets and were making tough decisions on continuing these services.

Another thing that might make our readers a little more comfortable, living in West Virginia, is the weather that Cleveland area residents endure. With Lake Erie to the North, the "lake effect" snow and wind is something that residents live with each winter. On a recent visit, the wind was blowing off the frozen lake and the snow had developed into blizzard conditions. It made me long for the relatively moderate climate in West Virginia.

So, if you have an opportunity to visit Cleveland, take some time to drive around the many cities and towns that surround Cleveland. You will see a wide variety of things in these quaint cities that might be good ideas for our area. Also, visit some of the restaurants and sights in the City of Cleveland.

My good friend, Matt Zone, a councilman in Cleveland

and the incoming President of the National League of Cities, represents an eclectic neighborhood that features a vibrant arts community with shops and eateries. The good things happening in Councilman Zone's district have not come easily but they have rallied the citizens to keep things moving in a positive direction, even in the face of challenges. One exciting development that comes in the wake of the Cleveland Cavaliers winning the NBA Championship, is LeBron James producing a television show called *Cleveland Hustles* in Matt's council district. This is giving Cleveland a great boost and leverages the powerful publicity that someone like LeBron James commands.

An additional benefit that comes with this type of national publicity is that it impacts the entire Northeastern part of Ohio. Indeed, since LeBron was born in Akron, his influence is also being felt in his hometown. You can't always count on your team winning a national championship but when it happens, take advantage of it!

Columbia, Missouri

"In Missouri, where I come from, we don't talk about
what we do - we just do it. If we talk about it, it's seen as
bragging."
Brad Pitt

Flying into St. Louis and hopping onto a shuttle van
for my trip to Columbia, Missouri, I immediately
remembered another trip over forty years ago when I
left Clarksburg for Army Basic Training at Fort Leonard Wood, Missouri. I remembered that the land was
pretty flat and the roads were quite a bit straighter than
West Virginia. As we drove through O'Fallon, Missouri,
I looked ahead and it was getting blacker by the moment
with lighting striking in a line headed right for us. I then
remembered the tornado drills our drill sergeants made
sure we practiced each weak and the concrete buildings
on base where we were to take shelter. I was sitting
right behind the driver and asked him if we should pull
over. He laughed and said that if he pulled over for every
thunderstorm like this, he would never get anyone to
Columbia. Just like he said, we drove through the storm
and made it safely to Columbia.

Columbia, Missouri is located almost equally distanced between St. Louis and Kansas City and is the
home of the University of Missouri. It is the state's fourth
most populous city with a population of around 115,000
residents. Local residents refer to it as "CoMo". You are
never far from the influences of the University of Missouri with the "Black and Gold" colors flying just about

everywhere. The University has over 35,000 students and with two other sizable colleges in town, Columbia has a booming economy and a youthful feel. Add to that the approximately 9,000 employees at the University of Missouri and it is easy to see why Columbia is one of the fastest growing cities in the country.

The downtown district in Columbia is a vibrant mix of restaurants, bars, small shops and interesting art galleries. The city has invested in attractive benches and other streetscape improvements that give the downtown a welcoming look and encourages people to walk around and visit the various attractions. They have also done something that I have seen in Los Angeles and a few other cities in my travels. The large metal utility boxes that are attached to the utility poles in almost every city are often a place that attracts graffiti or stickers and placards that gives the area a less than attractive look. Columbia has engaged artists to paint very attractive works of art on these boxes. They each are done in a different style and are really a nice addition to the Downtown. They have also installed attractive "bulletin boards" at various places on the sidewalks to allow the inevitable posting of events and other things that college students use to make announcements.

The Columbia City Hall is right in the middle of the downtown district and is an impressive building. The building, originally built as a hotel, underwent an extensive renovation and expansion several years ago. It is an excellent example of maintaining the integrity of the original design while creating a new and modern physical plant. The council chambers are large and can accommodate several hundred people. There is a large area as you enter the building that has tables and chairs and an information desk. After visiting over 500 city halls in my career, Columbia's is high on my list for attractiveness and functionality. I also liked the large letters on the front of the building that identified "City of Columbia".

I look forward to my next trip to "CoMo" and appreciate the hospitality of the City Staff, Mayor and Council. So long to this Amazing City!

Detroit, Michigan

"Go where you're celebrated, not tolerated. I'm celebrated in Detroit."
Kid Rock

After my recent trip to Chicago, we headed up to Detroit to meet with the Mayor of Detroit's Chief of Staff. I've always enjoyed flying into Detroit because the Detroit Metropolitan Wayne County Airport is one of my favorite airports. It is regularly ranked as one of the best airports in America and has many modern features that get you through the airport with ease.

We stayed at the historic Dearborn Inn, near the airport, which is built on the grounds of the Ford Motor Company. The hotel was built in 1931 and sits on twenty-three beautifully landscaped acres. Henry Ford commissioned the building of the hotel in order to have accommodations for visitors who flew in to his airport making it one of the first "airport hotels" in the country.

As we drove into downtown Detroit for our meeting, I was struck by the beautiful skyline and modern skyscrapers of the "Motor City". This differed from the many stories of burnt out buildings and urban blight that many people feel is the story of Detroit. Detroit is, indeed, dealing with many financial issues and the population has decreased dramatically in the past fifteen years. There are still nearly 700,000 citizens that live in the City of Detroit. It remains a center of financial and manufacturing activity in the state of Michigan. As we parked near the Detroit City Hall, it felt like you were in a vibrant and modern city poised for the future.

Our meeting with Alexis Wiley, the Mayor's Chief of Staff was very informative. We learned of the many exciting projects that may bring the Motor City back to the glory of old. Wiley, a former television news reporter is a bundle of energy and gets you feeling positive about the new Mayor and the city. We talked at length about the challenge of providing quality services to the citizens with high unemployment and a shrinking tax base. As we were wrapping up our meeting, Mayor Mike Duggan stuck his head in the door and we got to meet the man in charge of the revitalization of Detroit. Mayor Duggan is a lawyer and businessman who formerly was the CEO of Detroit Medical Center. He ran on a slogan of "Every Neighborhood Has a Future" championing a platform of economic turnaround, crime reduction and economic development.

Detroit is trying a multitude of ideas to inject vitality into neighborhoods including providing homes to artists if they will commit to living in the city and becoming active in the neighborhood. They are also working to 'light' up the city with new, energy efficient LED street-lights. The new lights are designed to provide a safer environment in the neighborhoods and reduce crime. These and other initiatives are designed to fulfill the Mayor's promise to address the crime and deterioration in the neighborhoods.

The history of Detroit is the story of one of the most progressive times in American history. It is a time of innovation and celebration of the American worker. It is the history of "Motown" and the "Supremes" and some of the best music ever produced. While many people seem to have written off the city of Detroit, a dedicated group of city officials are working hard to bring back this important part of our nation's history.

I'm betting on the future of Detroit. With a modern airport, a beautiful skyline and a new mayor, Detroit can once again be an Amazing City in our country.

Dublin, Ireland

"Fabulous place, Dublin is. The trouble is, you work hard and in Dublin you play hard as well."
Bonnie Tyler

I have wanted to visit Ireland for a long time. I was recently invited to meet with the Lord Mayor of Dublin, Ireland and city officials in Belfast, Northern Ireland, so I thought that this would be a chance to fulfill my wish list. My wife was also excited about the prospect of visiting Ireland, as her ancestors came from County Cork and Waterford in Ireland. Planning the trip was interesting, as I needed to coordinate our travel around the schedules of the city officials in Dublin and Belfast. I checked out hotels online and visited their websites to determine the distance from the city hall and other sights that we were interested in visiting.

I have found that having a positive attitude is the best way to enjoy travel whether in the United States or overseas. Travel is often unpredictable and can stress even the most stress-free individuals. When you look for the good in every experience and have a welcoming spirit, things happen that make even the toughest trip memorable.

Since we were leaving in the late afternoon, we drove to Pittsburgh and arrived at the airport in plenty of time for our 6:30 p.m. flight. As we sat in the gate area, we noticed that our flight was being delayed for about 15 minutes. This didn't bother us as we had plenty of time for our connecting flight in Philadelphia. Unfortunately, the flight delay increased and we started to get a little worried. We left Pittsburgh with just enough time to make our flight to Dublin. A quick trot through the Philadelphia Airport and we arrived at the American Airlines gate as they were announcing the boarding for Dublin.

The flight from Philadelphia to Dublin, Ireland is just a little over six hours. After we got seated and had dinner, we were well into the trip. Time seemed to pass pretty quickly. I was seated next to a young fellow from Galway who was returning home from Boston. He sold medical devices and traveled quite a bit for his job. He had five children and gave me a little information about life in Ireland. About an hour from landing, we got our first glimpse of Ireland. The green fields dotted with little cottages were everywhere. There were also large fields with bright yellow flowers that stood out, even from 26,000 feet. We learned that they are called "rape-seed" and are used to make cooking oil and biodiesel fuel. After a smooth landing, we were walking up the jet bridge and ready to explore the "Emerald Isle".

As we got in the cab for our trip to the hotel in Dublin, we immediately saw that the traffic direction was a good bit different than the United States. The cars have the steering wheels on the right hand side of the car and they drive to the left on the roads, the exact opposite of back home. Our driver spoke with a thick Irish accent and we had to ask him to repeat himself several times. We arrived at the Grand Canal Hotel, which naturally is located along what is known as the Grand Canal. The hotel was very nice and they had a room ready for us even though we arrived at just after 9:00 a.m.

We went to the room and got everything unpacked.

After a quick shower, we decided to take a walk around the neighborhood to get a feel for the area. We took off walking towards the Aviva Stadium, which is a huge soccer stadium right in the middle of a quiet residential neighborhood. It is relatively new and is located at a train station, which explains how so many people can access it without much parking. The houses along the way were attached brick townhouses with a small gravel pad in the front yard for parking. The one thing that stood out on each of the homes was the colorful door with a doorknob in the center of the door. Each home had a different color door and it made for an interesting neighborhood. As we walked more, we saw many more doors throughout the city with a distinctive color on each of them. The neighborhoods were very clean and well kept. There was some occasional graffiti but not out of the ordinary for a larger city like Dublin.

While you read about the pubs in Ireland, it is unbelievable how many are located throughout the entire country. Each pub has a distinctive name and there is generally a good crowd in each. At night, the crowd moves out onto the sidewalks and sometimes the streets. We learned that pubs are a large economic force in Ireland. They account for a large number of employees and a large contribution to the tax base. Tourists make up only 25% of the visitors to the pubs, so the locals are the mainstay of business.

Dublin is a very walkable city and we regularly walked six or more miles per day seeing the sights. Our hotel was about a fifteen minute walk from the city center and it helped to walk off some of the wonderful meals that we enjoyed in the city. Dublin recently installed a bike rental program that is popular in many cities around the United States. The bikes are parked at stations along the roads and can be rented by using a credit card. You can ride the bikes for free for the first thirty minutes and you are able to drop the bike off at another station, which makes it a convenient method of travel in the city.

There are many interesting things to see and do in Dublin. We took in many of the popular sights and could have stayed a month or more without seeing all that was of interest. Trinity College is one stop on everyone's list. It is a historic college that many famous Irish writers and poets attended. The grounds of the college are beautiful and are open to the public. One evening we walked around the campus and enjoyed a cricket practice on the huge practice fields in the center of the walled in campus. We also spent some time in the large public parks that are throughout Dublin. St. Stephen's Green is one of the more famous and is a beautiful spot to watch the swans swimming in the large lake. It is very peaceful and families with children are frequent visitors to the park.

Dublin has so much history that it is hard to even get a taste of it in a visit lasting a week or two. We felt blessed to spend some time in Dublin and look forward to a longer stay in the future.

Over my many years in local government I have had the opportunity to meet Mayors from throughout the United States and many cities around the world. In doing so, I have always been fascinated by the long history of mayors in Great Britain and Ireland. They are addressed as "Lord Mayor" and wear a large gold necklace, known as the Great Chain that would make any rap star jealous. I was invited to meet Lord Mayor

Christy Burke of Dublin to discuss innovative technologies from the United States that might be of interest to Dublin and also to see if there were things happening in Dublin that might be of use in U.S. cities.

We were asked to meet Lord Mayor Burke at the Mansion House, the official residence of the Lord Mayor. The Lord Mayor is elected for a one-year term and can live in the historic Mansion House during their term of office. The Mansion House is a beautiful house that was built between 1705 and 1710 by a developer who constructed the house for his mistress. She did not like the house and never moved in, thereby leaving the wealthy developer with an unused house. He offered it for sale to the city of Dublin and they purchased it for the sum of approximately 3,500 pounds. Over the years, the house has played a large role in Irish history with many significant meetings held within.

We were greeted by the curator of the house and led to the Drawing Room to wait for our meeting with the Lord Mayor. We were offered tea and pastries and felt like royalty as we awaited our meeting. Mr. Michael Sands, the International relations director for the City of Dublin arrived first and briefed us on the schedule and the topics of discussions. He also gave us a brief history of the Mansion House and described some of the portraits hanging on the walls of the reception room. At the appointed hour, the Lord Mayor arrived and greeted us to his home. Lord Mayor Christy Burke is an affable man and launched right into a discussion about the city of Dublin and all of the exciting things happening. He explained that the city has been very involved in energy efficiency and that the city council had made many investments in public-private partnerships to address climate change. Transit is also important to the city council and they have supported many of the transit projects currently under construction in the city center. The Lord Mayor was especially proud of the bicycle rental program and told how they enacted changes to speed up the usage of the bicycle program.

After the Lord Mayor left, Mr. Michael Sands gave us a tour of the Mansion House and arranged for us to visit the Dublin City Hall and the Dublin Castle. Michael also told us about an event next year for all of the U.S. cities who have sister city relationships with Dublin. The mayors from each of those cities will be invited to Dublin to participate in a ceremony to recognize the value of working together to share cultures and ideas

As we finished our tour of the Mansion House, Michael pointed out one last item in the house that he said we should find interesting. It was an oak bar with a beer tap for all of the products of the Guinness Brewery. He explained that the founder of the Guinness Company had served as Lord Mayor and promised to provide as much beer as needed to the city at no charge. He said that they have kept that promise over many decades and each week new kegs of beer are delivered to the Mansion House for events and personal use of the Lord Mayor. I'm thinking that this is one idea I can bring back to U.S. cities that will be warmly received.

Ireland is one of the most beautiful countries in the world and the trip to the Burren and the Cliffs of Moher was a highlight of our visit. As we prepared to head to Northern Ireland, we hated to say goodbye to such a welcoming and beautiful country.

Durban, South Africa

"Our daily deeds as ordinary South Africans must produce an actual South African reality that will reinforce humanity's belief in justice, strengthen its confidence in the nobility of the human soul, and sustain all our hopes for a glorious life for all."

Nelson Mandela

I n 2011, I was asked to represent the National League of Cities at the signing of a historic Memorandum of Understanding between the South Africa Local Government Association (SALGA) and the National League of Cities (NLC), the United States' oldest and largest organization devoted to strengthening and promoting cities. Ms. Rita Jo Lewis of the United States State Department witnessed the event representing Secretary of State Hilary Clinton. I traveled with my good friend, Alderman Joe Davis of Milwaukee, Wisconsin and his wife who is a native of South Africa. Visiting South Africa had been on my bucket list for a long time and I was excited as I made my preparations to leave.

Traveling to South Africa is quite a journey. We left Washington, DC and flew for ten hours to Dakar, Senegal. I figured that since we were in Africa it would be a short hop to Durban, South Africa but I was mistaken. As the plane took off from Senegal, I asked the flight attendant how long the flight to Durban would take. She smiled and said, "Ten hours." I got a lesson on how large the continent of Africa is and learned that the entire United States, China, Mexico, India and Eastern

Europe could fit into the land space of Africa. South Africa is the 25ᵗʰ largest country in the world and has over 53 million people.

I had known of South Africa as the homeland of Nelson Mandela and from movies like *Invictus* that told the story of the 1995 South African Rugby World Cup team that united the apartheid-torn land. The history of South Africa is one of colonial occupation from as early as 1652 and an often-violent oppression. The discovery of diamonds in 1867 and gold in 1884 started the Mineral Revolution and intensified the European colonialist's efforts to gain control over the indigenous peoples. In 1948, segregation began under Dutch and British colonial rule. The Nationalist Government classified all peoples into three races and developed rights and limitations for each. This legally institutionalized segregation became known as apartheid. The whites enjoyed the highest standard of living in all of Africa, comparable to First World Western nations while blacks remained disadvantaged in almost every standard, including income, housing, education and life expectancy.

Nelson Mandela emerged as a prominent figure in South Africa during the apartheid period and was a member of the African National Congress (ANC). He was trained as a lawyer and became involved with groups that were fighting apartheid. In 1964, Mandela was arrested and tried for his work against the Nationalist Government and sentenced to life imprisonment. He was imprisoned at Robben Island from 1964 to 1982 and led a difficult life working in a lime quarry. He was forbidden to wear sunglasses and the glare from the lime permanently damaged his eyesight. He was allowed one letter and one visit every six months and was often harassed and physically abused by the white prison wardens.

In 1989, following the fall of the Berlin Wall, F.W. de Klerk, the head of the National Party, met with Mandela and discussed releasing him and legalizing the formerly banned political parties. He was released from custody on February 2, 1990. Mandela became an international figure and traveled throughout South Africa and the world speaking out about apartheid and injustice. His following increased and in 1994 he was elected as the President of South Africa.

While South Africa still struggles with many economic and political issues, they are working to develop a peaceful transition from apartheid to democratic government. AIDS has devastated the country. It is estimated that there are over 6.3 million people living with HIV, more than any other country in the world. The HIV/AIDS infection in South Africa is divided along racial lines with 13.6% of blacks who are HIV-positive while only .3% of whites have the disease.

As our plane touched down in Durban, I knew that this trip would be one that I would remember for a long time.

After twenty hours in the air, I was ready to be on land and start exploring Durban, South Africa. Durban is a modern city and is the largest city in the South African province of KwaZulu-Natal with over 3.5 million citizens. It is located on the Indian Ocean and is the largest municipality on the coast of the African Continent. Durban is a large tourist center due in part to the beautiful beaches that line the coast. As we walked along the beach, I remarked that if we had landed in Miami, we would not have noticed much difference.

A highlight of the visit to Durban was going to the top of Moses Mabhida Stadium. The stadium was constructed for the FIFA World Cup, which was held in South Africa at several venues. The stadium seats 62,760 spectators and has a large arch that is 348 feet over the field. We traveled to the top of the stadium in a tram-like vehicle that climbs along rails. The view was spectacular and we could see for miles in all directions. The waves hitting the uShaka Beach were beautiful. Our guide explained that in 2011, they installed a large cable to the arch and allowed people to jump off the top of the stadium and swing over the field. While it looked like fun, we declined to try this adventure.

We did get to visit some wildlife preserves and see some native dancing and storytelling. At one site, there were hundreds of crocodiles behind chain-link enclosures that did not seem nearly strong enough to keep these massive beasts contained. The size of the crocodiles was truly impressive and one huge crocodile was the star of the show. A young man went into the enclosure and used a long stick to agitate the croc to the enjoyment of the crowd. He was pretty nimble as he taunted the huge croc while talking to the crowd. The other attraction at this park was the snake area. Africa is home to some very deadly snakes and we got to see many of the most dangerous, including the Black Mamba, thought to be the deadliest snake in the world. Everything was going great until the attendant brought out some snakes to let the crowd experience the feeling of holding a snake. It was somewhat embarrassing to see little kids letting the snakes crawl all over them while most of our group was running for the gate. I did hold one of the snakes for a quick picture but it was not the most enjoyable part of the visit.

Durban relies on the tourist industry for a large part of its economy and visitors are not disappointed. In addition to the wildlife parks and sporting venues, there is also a large casino along the beach that attracts visitors from all over the world. Golf is also a popular reason that people visit the area. With world famous golfers like Gary Player and Ernie Els, South Africa hosts many popular golf tournaments with large numbers of visitors.

All in all, Durban is a beautiful city with a diverse population and many things to do. The beaches are fantastic and the climate is among the best in Africa. I did not envision such a modern city but it was a pleasant surprise.

Durham, North Carolina

"When I was a young boy, growing up in Durham, North Carolina, the women in my family were truly passionate about their clothes; nothing was more beautiful to me than women dressing with the utmost, meticulous attention to accessories, shoes, handbags, hats, coats, dresses and gloves to attend Sunday church services."
Andre Leon Talley

I had the opportunity to travel recently to Durham, North Carolina to speak to the participants in the America's Best Communities competition which features fifteen cities vying for over $10 Million dollars in prize money. The program was very interesting and reminded me of the America's Got Talent show since each of the communities had to present a ten-minute speech about their community. County singer Vince Gill was serving as the ambassador for the competition and it was nice getting to meet him and enjoy the Durham area. Durham is a very interesting city with a rich history as a tobacco processor during the last century.

The tobacco industry is fading in importance in the United States economy but it once had a huge impact and provided thousands of jobs throughout the South. One of the places that had a prominent role in this industry is Durham, North Carolina. The remnants of this once powerful industry are evident as you walk through the downtown. The American Tobacco Company factory is now a hotbed of activity with restaurants, stores and businesses housed in the buildings that previously produced billions of cigarettes and other tobacco products. A large smokestack still has the Lucky Strike emblem emblazoned on the side and murals highlight some of the other brands that were once a part of our daily life. Durham has rebounded from the decline of the tobacco industry and is now a part of what is called the "Research Triangle", composed of Durham, Raleigh, Cary and Chapel Hill. The presence of Duke, North Carolina State and the University of North Carolina provide a foundation for research and the educated workforce employed in many of the high-tech companies that have located in this region.

Durham has around 250,000 citizens and is part of a region that has over 2 million residents. The biggest employer is Duke University and the Duke University Health System with over 35,000 employees. Duke currently has around 14,000 students. They attend classes on the 8,600 acre campus that is located about two miles from the downtown. North Carolina Central University is also housed in Durham and has a student body of close to 10,000 students. It is a historically Black university and was established in 1910.

Durham has a minor league baseball team named the "Durham Bulls". They play in the newly built downtown baseball stadium. Going to the baseball games are a great family activity and the Durham Bulls set a single season attendance record of 554,788 fans in 2015. The Durham Bulls became internationally famous following the release of the 1988 film called *Bull Durham* starring Kevin Costner, Tim Robbins and Susan Sarandon. The Durham Bulls are a Triple-A team with an affiliation to the Major League Tampa Bay Rays.

It is not hard to find something to do in Durham with

baseball, Duke Basketball and Football, and dozens of other venues that provide entertainment and culture. There are very colorful murals around the downtown as Durham has embraced public art in many large and small ways. The city has worked hard to reduce crime in the city and the downtown is now considered very safe with a healthy nightlife.

As I headed to the Raleigh-Durham Airport, I had a nice conversation with my very pleasant limo driver who told me how much she enjoyed living in Durham. She was from Morocco and is in pre-med school, in addition to driving the limo. She said the only thing she finds bad about Durham is the traffic. I guess that might be expected from someone who has to deal with it every day!

All in all, Durham is an exciting city with a lot of jobs and a moderate climate which seems to suit just about everyone I met.

Florence, Italy

"Italy will never be a normal country. Because Italy is Italy. If we were a normal country, we wouldn't have Rome. We wouldn't have Florence. We wouldn't have the marvel that is Venice."
Matteo Renzi

In 2011, I attended a meeting of the World Council of the United Cities and Local Governments (UCLG) in the city of Florence, Italy. I had read about Florence for many years and everything that I heard was of a beautiful city with unequaled art and memorable sites. Florence is the capital city of the Italian region of Tuscany. It is the most populous city in Tuscany with a metropolitan region of over 1.5 million residents. We arrived at the Baglioni Hotel and got settled before we headed out to explore the city. The hotel was built in 1903 and was just a short distance from the Palazzo del Congressi, the exhibition center where our meetings were to be held. The rooms were very nice with a beautiful view of the skyline of the city.

Walking towards the center of the city, I caught a glimpse of one of the most beautiful buildings I had ever seen. It was the Cathedral of Saint Mary of the Flower and is a stunning structure faced with shades of green and pink marble. The cathedral was begun in 1296 and completed in 1436. For centuries, the dome atop the cathedral was the largest in the world and is still the largest brick dome ever constructed. You enter the building through massive wooden doors and the beauty continues inside. The interior is unbelievably high and makes you question how they could have constructed such a building centuries ago.

Florence has a large amount of artwork and statues throughout the city. From the copy of Michelangelo's *David* in the Piazza della to the beautiful *Fountain of Neptune* situated on the Piazza della Signoria (Signoria Square). There are also many public parks and plazas for visitors to rest and enjoy the atmosphere of the city.

Street performers are a common site throughout the city. While many cities have street performers, Florence has taken it to a new level. One performer was dressed as a street sweeper. As you walked by you were convinced that it was a statue made of marble. Suddenly, he would move his broom and children and adults alike would jump and smile.

One of the most beautiful sights in the city is the *Ponte Vecchio* (Old Bridge) that spans the Arno River. The bridge is lined with shops and is a popular tourist attraction in the city. At any time, there are dozens of artists sketching the bridge. It is one of the most iconic views in the city. The bridge also carries the elevated corridor linking the Uffizi to the Medici residence. Our group was honored to visit some of the famous museums and we walked along the elevated corridor, which was a rare treat for visitors to Florence. It is hard to describe the thousands of paintings and sculptures that line the walls. It would take months to fully appreciate the amount of history that is contained in these works of art.

As the meetings for the UCLG commenced, they held a grand reception to welcome the delegates to the city. A group of colorfully uniformed men played long trumpets as they announced the arrival of the Mayor of Florence, Matteo Renzi. Mayor Renzi is a very dynamic person and mingled with the delegates, greeting each one. I spent some time with him and related that my city of Clarksburg, West Virginia has a large Italian population and celebrates the West Virginia Italian Festival each year. I was pleasantly surprised that Mayor Renzi assumed the office of Prime Minister of Italy on February 22, 2014. He became the youngest person, at 39, to become Prime Minister since 1861.

My visit to Florence gave me an appreciation of art and how it can define a city. Art lovers by the millions are drawn to Florence and it provides a large impact to the economy. I also liked the beautiful public squares and green spaces which provide room for visitors and small businesses. Cities in the United States could learn a lot by visiting Florence and seeing how art makes Florence an Amazing City!

Fort Lauderdale, Florida

"Don't grow up too quickly, lest you forget how much you love the beach."
Michelle Held

Getting invited to speak at a conference in Fort Lauderdale in late October is any speaker's dream assignment and staying in a resort on the beach was an extra special treat. Fort Lauderdale is a beautiful city and offers a lot of amenities to residents and tourists alike. Greater Fort Lauderdale has over 4,000 restaurants, 63 golf courses, 12 shopping malls, 16 museums, 132 nightclubs, 278 parkland campsites, and 100 marinas housing 45,000 resident yachts. I was invited to speak at the Alliance for Innovation's "Big Ideas" conference that focuses on building resilient cities. The Conference is an "invitation only" event and draws a talented group of city managers, city staff, authors and other thought leaders from throughout the country.

Thanks to the wonder of the Internet, my good friend, former Mayor Jim Naugle, learned that I was visiting his city via Facebook and invited me to lunch. Jim served as Mayor of Fort Lauderdale for twenty-four years and we became good friends, as we both were involved with the National League of Cities. Jim left office six years ago and now works in the busy Fort Lauderdale real estate market. Jim does a lot of work with people involved in the boating industry and sells commercial properties as well as homes. We had lunch at the Lauderdale Yacht Club. It is located along the Intracoastal Waterway and is the meeting place for many of the movers and shakers in the city. The food was delicious and after lunch we took a quick tour of the city. One benefit of touring the city with a long time Mayor is that you get to hear the inside story on many of projects and developments.

The Fort Lauderdale Boat Show is one of the exciting things that has grown into a booming part of the economy. The show attracts thousands of visitors to the city and has a larger economic impact than the Super Bowl. The number of multi-million dollar yachts is truly amazing. Naturally, the weather is one of Fort Lauderdale's biggest draws and people come from throughout the world to enjoy the beaches that stretch from one end of the city to the other. I was a little worried that I would miss the sun as it was a little windy and overcast the day I arrived but the sun came out the next day and it was beautiful.

The conference was stimulating. I learned a lot and met some very talented people. Fort Lauderdale City Manager Lee Feldman served as host for the event and did a great job of providing a lot of content, combined with showing off his city. Current Mayor, John P. "Jack" Seiler, welcomed the group and talked about the future of the city and some exciting projects that were being planned. One of the most exciting projects is a rail line that will run from Fort Lauderdale to Orlando. Fort Lauderdale is definitely an Amazing City and one that should be on everyone's list for a visit.

Hajduboszomeny, Hungary

"In Hungary all native music, in its origin, is divided naturally into melody destined for song or melody for the dance."
Franz Liszt

Without a doubt, the city that I have visited with the longest name is Hajduboszomeny, Hungary. I visited Hajduboszomeny as part of the Habitat for Humanity Global Village Program. Our mission was to build some modest houses for residents of the town. The town reminded me of Salem, West Virginia in both size and character. The Global Village Program brings people together from throughout the United States and other countries to build in one of the many countries that have a Habitat affiliate. My daughter, Sarah joined me for this visit and it made for an unforgettable father-daughter experience.

On our first couple of days we encountered a delightful young lady named Erica from Hajduboszomeny, who was 17 and heard that there were a group of English speaking people in town. She said that she wanted to practice her English and showed up each day to put in a hard day's work. I was so impressed with her and admired her drive and determination. She eventually brought her brother, mother and father to the worksite. We enjoyed getting to know them and hear about their life.

Our accommodations for the two-week adventure was

a spa type camp that featured mud baths and cold and hot spring pools. This was unusual since generally the Global Village program uses spartan accommodations, often with outdoor toilets.

Needless to say, no one was complaining about the fortunate break we encountered. We would have a nice breakfast and take a bag lunch to the worksite which was about 20 minutes from the camp. We decided we would work in the morning, take a two-hour lunch and work longer in the afternoon. This allowed us to return to the spa and take a delightful soak in the hot spring water encased in smooth mud. A quick shower and we headed back to the worksite refreshed and ready for action.

While many people have asked me why I would travel across the world to build houses, I must say that I believe this is the best way to travel. You get to experience people of another culture and language in their home and not just driving by in an oversized tour bus. It is also amazing how the workday goes by so quickly. Sitting around at dinner or having an evening drink in a pub becomes the most memorable part of the day.

The highlight of the trip was "Gulyas" (Goulash), a traditional dinner which features a huge iron pot that is filled with an array of potatoes and special ingredients simmered over a wood fire. All of the families that were in line to receive the houses came with their children. We were seated on wooden benches listening to Hungarian music and doing traditional dances. Several times over the course of the evening we would spy the families looking at the foundation for their future homes. The children would walk over to their bedrooms and sit on the ground and imagine what it would be like to finally have a decent home. It was hard to hold back the tears as we saw the smiles on the family's faces.

I stay in touch with several people who were on the trip and I regularly email Erica to see how her life is progressing. I am hopeful that my contribution provided a better life for some disadvantaged families in a country far away and that they might remember the big guy and his daughter who visited and pounded a few nails many years ago!

Huntington, West Virginia

"Make no little plans; they have no magic to stir men's blood and probably themselves will not be realized."
Daniel Burnham

Effective leadership can do great things in turning a city from great to Amazing. One such example is Mayor Steve Williams in Huntington, West Virginia. I met Mayor Williams shortly after his election as Huntington's 47th Mayor at a West Virginia Municipal League Conference. He was full of ideas but willing to listen to others for ways to improve the city while dealing with an assortment of problems including a severe drug problem which had created a negative image for the home of Marshall University. Mayor Williams recently made national news for a video he made addressing the problem of drugs in the city. His video was a call for prayer to heal the drug abusers, to protect the police and to deliver the drug dealers from their life of crime. While originally targeted to local ministers, the video went viral and had hundreds of thousands of "hits" from throughout the world. The Mayor realizes that the drug problem will not be solved by prayer alone. He has added police personnel and worked with providers of drug treatment to give abusers a path to recovery.

Huntington is also the home to Marshall University and Mayor Williams has taken a personal approach to cleaning up the properties surrounding the campus of the university. One particularly troublesome problem is one that plagues many college towns including Morgantown, home to West Virginia University. That is the littering of properties after a weekend of parties and football games. Red cups and other trash litter the main thoroughfare driven by many residents on their way to Sunday church services. The Mayor took to the streets and requested a meeting with the presidents of the fraternity houses which seemed to be the worst offenders when it came to littering. He suggested that the fraternities have their pledges clean up the yards after the parties on Saturday night. After some initial reluctance, the fraternity leaders chose to clean up rather than to face the stiff penalties suggested by the Mayor.

One thing that I immediately liked about the Mayor was his consistently positive attitude. He speaks in positive terms and has changed the mood from pessimism to enthusiastic optimism. He has chided city staff for repeating the oft-heard phrase, "financially troubled Huntington" which had become part of the city's identification. He also started to pay attention to detail. Flowers at the entrances to the city and regular street cleaning have paid dividends in associating a clean and attractive image to the city.

City Hall is part of the transformation of the city. The building, which was built at the turn of the century, is clean and freshly painted. Projects are planned to improve the windows and restore the façade to its original grandeur. A pleasant surprise in the City Hall building is a large auditorium on the second floor. The facility seats several hundred patrons and has been used recently as the site of a high school prom.

I predict that we will see some Amazing things coming

from the city of Huntington, West Virginia. A dynamic Mayor and a positive outlook are hard to beat. It seems that the Mayor's positive attitude has even rubbed off on the Marshall football team as they start the season unbeaten and ranked in the national standings.

Huntsville, Alabama

"You can say a lot of bad things about Alabama, but you can't say Alabamans as a people are unduly afraid of deep fryers. In that first week at the Creek, the cafeteria served fried chicken, chicken fried steak, and fried okra, which marked my first foray into the delicacy that is the fried vegetable."
John Green

Huntsville, Alabama is called "The Rocket City" for its close association with the United States Space Program. As you drive into town, you cannot miss the display of historic rockets in Rocket Park on the grounds of the U.S. Space and Rocket Center. The city has around 185,000 residents within the city limits and over 417,000 people residing in the immediate area. The city was the first to be incorporated in Alabama in 1811. It was named after John Hunt who was a Revolutionary War veteran who settled in the area in 1805.

I was visiting Huntsville to speak at the annual conference of the Alabama League of Municipalities which was holding its conference at the Von Braun Center. As I arrived from my flight, I was met by a Huntsville policeman who was assigned to get me to the hotel. It is always nice to meet city employees and get their insight into the area. On our drive to the hotel, Donny told me that his father was a Huntsville policeman and his son is currently on the force. He was quite positive about the city and pointed out a lot of the new construction in the downtown. He explained that crime was about average for a mid-sized city like Huntsville but he was quick to point out that the city was considered safe as long as you used good sense.

My hotel was adjacent to the Von Braun Center. As I checked in I saw a full sized "astronaut" in the lobby. After a quick "selfie" with the space traveler, I went over to the conference center to register. I had spoken at the Von Braun Center several years ago but they have done a tremendous renovation in the past several years and it is quite impressive. I walked around the outside where they have developed a beautiful park with walkways and water fountains that spray high into the air. They also have Koi fish in the water. The bright gold of the fish shines through the water and is an impressive sight. The area is close to downtown and there were many people eating their lunches and relaxing on the comfortable benches.

An unusual feature of the Huntsville area is the fact that the City of Huntsville totally surrounds another city. Madison, Alabama is a city of 42,000 residents and was originally known as Madison Station due to it being a stop on the Memphis & Charleston Railroad. My good friend, Cynthia McCollum was a councilmember in Madison when she served as President of the National League of Cities. I was fortunate to get to see her at the President's Banquet during the conference. While I have heard of instances of a city being totally surrounded by another city, this is a pretty rare occurrence in the United States.

The economy of Huntsville, while still dependent on the space industry, is working to become more diversified. Second term Mayor Tommy Battle has done a great job leading the effort to bring regional leaders together to recruit new industry and improve education opportunities for the workforce. As a result of his work, Huntsville is leading the state in new jobs and economic investment.

After just a couple of days, I was being driven to the airport by another fine member of the Huntsville Police Department. He was a young officer and was quite excited to be serving the citizens. He informed me that the department had just been issued body cameras. He showed me how they worked, buckled to the front of his uniform. I was very impressed with his professionalism and enjoyed our conversation on the ride to the airport. My visit to Rocket City was much too brief but I enjoyed it nonetheless!

Indiana, Pennsylvania

"Indiana means home to me. It is a town for me to cling to, because my mother and father are here. I was born and reared here. I have a great love and pride for Indiana. I love every bit of it."
Jimmy Stewart

My last visit to Indiana, Pennsylvania was over thirty years ago when I attended an educational seminar at the Indiana University of Pennsylvania or IUP as it is known. On that visit, I don't remember spending much time exploring the city and I was glad I was able to revisit this quaint little town in Western Pennsylvania a few weeks ago. The drive to Indiana is very pleasant and passes a lot of small farms and countryside. I was attending a District Meeting of the Pennsylvania Municipal League. The Mayor of Indiana and the President of IUP were in attendance and spoke of their love for the city.

Indiana is a borough in the county seat of Indiana County and has about 14,000 citizens. They promote themselves as the "Christmas Tree Capital of the World" because the National Christmas Tree Growers Association was founded there. There are still a lot of Christmas tree farms in the area which contribute to the local economy. Coal mining was a major industry for many years but has declined recently with the downturn in the coal industry. By far, the largest employer is the University. They also account for additional jobs in the student housing and student services sector.

The most famous resident of Indiana was actor Jimmy Stewart who was born and lived there through high school before heading to Hollywood. The town has developed a museum to his memory on the third floor of the local library. They hold an annual film festival as part of the town's "It's a Wonderful Life" holiday celebration. A bronze statue of the actor was erected on his 75th birthday and stands in his honor at the county courthouse.

At the suggestion of the Mayor, I drove around the downtown area before I departed the morning following my speech. I was so impressed at the beautiful little town with shops and restaurants along the main street. They were replacing some of the sidewalks and putting in a new streetscape with historic light posts and trash receptacles. Almost every storefront was filled and many had small local businesses associated with the arts. They had also just finished a beautiful arched area with metal tables and benches along the sidewalks that served as a great place for residents and students to sit during the day and early evening. The street furniture had plaques attached with the names of those who donated towards the installation. This is always a good idea and encourages a feeling of ownership among the residents.

Indiana, PA is one of the best examples in the country of a small town that has made the most of its relationship with the local college. Town-Gown relationships are often difficult but when they work, they can be a huge benefit to both the city and the university. There is a large amount of construction going on in the city and much of it is related to student housing. The Kovalchick Convention and Athletic Complex is one of the newest buildings and has a new hotel being constructed next door.

It is easy to see why the residents of Indiana are generally smiling when you greet them on the street. It could have been the setting for *It's A Wonderful Life* and knowing that Jimmy Stewart walked these streets makes Indiana one of the most Amazing small towns in America!

Jeju Island, South Korea

"My dream is to go spend a week on some island with no phone."
Cara Delevingne

In all of my travels, one place that stands out is Jeju Island, South Korea. I was invited to speak at a session of the United Cities and Local Government World Conference a few years ago. I was excited to visit a place that seemed cloaked in mystery and enchantment. Jeju Island, a volcanic island located in the Korean Strait, is a popular tourist destination with thousands of visitors annually. It is on the UNESCO, World Heritage Site and is filled with volcanic rock structures and a shoreline with beautiful lava tubes formed when the molten lava hit the ocean water. Over 10 million visitors were attracted to the island in 2013 and it is quickly becoming the Hawaii of South Korea.

The food of Jeju Island was quite different from anything I had experienced before. There were open food markets with fresh fish and mounds of vegetables, spices and all sorts of fruit. Restaurants featured the traditional South Korean dish of kimchi and soups that were spicy and delicious. Much of the seafood is obtained by the process of "free diving" in which ladies called *haenyos* dive without equipment for an assortment of delicacies from the sea. The women start diving at around age 11 and some will continue until over 65 years of age. Seeing these ladies huddled around the shoreline in rubber boots and raincoats is quite the site.

The island was recently in the news as it was the destination for the ferry which tragically overturned and killed over 300 passengers. Most were school children on holiday headed to Jeju Island. I remembered that on my trip to Jeju, there were hundreds of school children in their uniforms at almost every site. They were laughing and giggling. I can still see their faces, sweet and innocent. The sinking of the ferry was the worst ferry disaster in South Korea since another tragic accident in 1993. I felt so sorry for the parents and friends of these young people, who had probably visited Jeju in much the same way when they were young.

I enjoyed my visit to this beautiful island and hope to return some day. It is truly a treasure and the sights and sounds resonate in my head quite often. That is the true value of travel. You never lose the experience. It is placed in a special section of your brain that pops in to revisit these places whenever the fancy strikes. Good travels!

Johannesburg, South Africa

"When I came to Johannesburg from the countryside, I knew nobody, but many strangers were very kind to me. I then was dragged into politics, and then, subsequently, I became a lawyer."
Nelson Mandela

Johannesburg is a city of about four million inhabitants and is well known for vast quantizes of minerals, including gold and diamonds. The downtown area is a modern city with skyscrapers and shopping areas. The housing goes from very modern with large houses to areas of extreme poverty with tin and wooden shanties. Driving around the city, you notice super-highways that remind you of larger cities in the United States. After the end of apartheid, the city struggled to operate services primarily funded by the wealthier neighborhoods and to control crime. The city services have improved but still need investment to provide infrastructure to the entire city.

While not a large tourist destination, Johannesburg is a transit point for connecting flights to Cape Town, Durban and the Kruger National Park. New museums and other attractions have been developed to take advantage of visitors passing through. A lot of visitors enjoy the wildlife reserves and zoos in the area. Much attention is paid to endangered species and several reserves are dedicated to preserving cheetahs, rhino and lions.

Sports are popular and soccer is comparable to the National Football League in the United States. Impressive stadiums are in many parts of the city as well as venues for cricket and rugby. It was common to see a group of young boys kicking a soccer ball in an empty field or along the roads. Running is also a popular sport and you see hundreds of people running along the highways in the cool mornings.

Johannesburg is home to a large amount of public art. Many prominent artists have done pieces of public art throughout the city. There is also a large amount of park space in the more affluent neighborhoods.

As part of our visit, we were invited for a briefing from the United States Embassy in Pretoria, the capital of South Africa. Pretoria is a short forty-five minute drive from Johannesburg. The embassy is a very large complex behind a wrought iron fence that surrounds nearly a complete city block. We met the U.S. Ambassador and took pictures in his office.

The staff of the embassy talked about their work in South Africa and how they interact with the South African officials. It was so interesting leaning how the diplomats attend various meetings with groups who are working with issues like trade and AIDS education. They monitor newspapers and media reports and meet with various officials throughout the country.

As our trip came to an end, we were waiting in the Durban Airport and saw some of the delegates who were attending the South Africa Local Government Association Conference. They were from a small village in South Africa. We struck up a conversation about issues that were important in their village. One lady mentioned that her village was getting a new water station.

I did not fully understand what a water station was and I asked her to explain it to me. She explained that they have a water well in one part of the village and the citizens bring bottles and buckets to fill with water since they do not have running water. Now their village will have a second water well for the citizens. She was so proud and I learned a little about how fortunate we are in the United States.

South Africa was an interesting place to visit and one where I learned so much about a part of the world where many people don't have the opportunity to visit. It was definitely a memorable visit to several Amazing Cities!

Key West, Florida

"If life gives you limes, make margaritas."
Jimmy Buffett

While I've written about my trips to Key West previously, there are always some new and exciting things happening that warrant another look. My wife and I have made five trips to Key West over the past twenty or so years. Each visit has caused us to fall in love with this tiny island over and over again. The weather is always pleasant and the people could not be nicer.

Packing for Key West is the easiest thing I have ever done. Two pair of shorts, three t-shirts, underwear and a swimsuit is all that is needed to survive for a few days or even a few months! The restaurants are all "beachwear" friendly and the weather is such that rarely do you need a jacket or sweatshirt. It is always nice to wear some "WVU" gear and you will surely be tapped on the shoulder by a fellow Mountaineer. We have never been there without seeing someone from West Virginia.

A popular place that we head to right after the plane lands is the Schooner Wharf Bar. This is the epitome of a beach hangout and they never seem to fail. The food is great and the margaritas hit the spot after a long day in the air. The resident performer is a fellow named Michael McCloud who happens to be from Beckley. He is a legend in the Keys. He smokes a cigarette and appears to be downing massive amounts of liquor but our cab driver told us that most of that is an act. He is a family man when he is not doing his show. For a five dollar tip he will sing "Country Roads" and acknowledge his Mountaineer heritage.

Our traveling companions on our ventures to Key West are our good friends, Pat and Lori Joyce of Bridge-port. We enjoy spending time with them and it never gets boring from morning till night. Pat and I enjoy a good cigar next to the pool and it is generally late into the night before we call it quits. We stay at the Harbor Inn which is a small bed and breakfast with about twenty rooms. It never feels crowded. The people we meet are always interesting and come from throughout the United States and abroad. Most of the people are regulars and visit each year.

One change that has occurred in Key West is the arrival of cruise ships. They built a dock and during the week there are one or two ships that arrive for the day. The streets are filled with cruise passengers buying sou-venirs and T-shirts before they have to get back on the ship. I'm sure that some people don't look at the cruise industry as a positive for Key West but it does put a lot of people on the streets supporting local merchants. We have found that even with the ships stopping during the day, the evenings are still filled with the character we have come to associate with Key West.

Because my work takes me to a lot of cities throughout the country and abroad, Key West remains my favorite vacation spot. It is easy to get to and the pace of life is as peaceful as anywhere in the world. If you are looking for a completely different vacation spot, try out Key West. I could go two or three times a year but I like to savor the experience. I hope I will never get tired of living like a beach bum for a week or two!

Krakow, Poland

I have a sweet tooth for song and music.
This is my Polish sin.
Pope John Paul II (Karol Wojtyla of Krakow)

In 2000, I decided to volunteer for the Habitat for Humanity Global Village Program, which is designed to build houses for the poor in various parts of the world. I had been involved with the Harrison County Chapter of Habitat for Humanity for several years and enjoyed building houses there. The thought of joining a group of volunteers from throughout the United States and Canada was exciting. I looked forward to seeing Poland, a country that I had studied in school. After filling out the various forms and making sure my passport was up-to-date, I left for a two-week adventure. We were to meet in Krakow for two days prior to traveling to the worksite in the city of Wroclaw. I had packed my bags with work clothes, boots and gloves in anticipation of the construction that we would soon be doing.

The work team was composed of a diverse group of people, many being young with about equal amounts of men and women. A farmer named Jerry from Iowa, a Yale graduate from San Francisco, a Korean girl from DC, a teacher from Canada and about a dozen other adventure seekers like me. As we arrived in Krakow, we introduced ourselves and had a group dinner when everyone was at the hotel. We then ventured out into Krakow to enjoy this historic city.

Krakow is the second largest and one of the oldest

cities in Poland. It has traditionally been one of the leading centers of Polish academic, cultural and artistic life and is a thriving economic hub. One of its most famous natives was Karol Wojityla, archbishop of Krakow who became Pope John Paul II. We visited the pope's home church. His image was seen in most stores and restaurants. In our short visit, we were able to see many of the sites that make this one of the most beautiful cities in the world. On each corner, there are beautiful churches of various architectural styles. As we visited each, we would remark how this was the most beautiful church we had ever seen until we walked to the next corner and were even more amazed at the next one. We also visited Wawel Castle; a beautiful red brick building that was built in the 10th Century.

I think my favorite part of the visit to Krakow was visiting the Main Market Square. It is a large open area surrounded by colorful buildings with dozens of outdoor restaurants and bars. We would sit at the restaurants and watch the people stroll about in the evening. The square is the center of social activity in Krakow. You would see people dressed in their finest clothes walking among the flower stands and street performers. Late one evening, we went to a jazz club that was located three stories below the street. As we walked down the narrow stairs, the smell of cigars and cigarettes filled the air. It felt like we were in an ancient cave and indeed, the walls were constructed of brick and had arched doorways with very low ceilings. The jazz group was tucked in a corner and the tables were crowded together with waiters sliding among the crowd. It was one of the most intriguing evenings I have ever spent, however I would admit that I kept looking at ways to escape in case of a fire!

Krakow was a great place to get to know the other team members as we prepared for two weeks of construction work. We bid farewell to this beautiful city as we boarded a small bus on our way to Wroclaw.

Laredo, Texas

"You haven't had food till you have lunch in the town of Laredo!"
Brian Davis

When I learned that I was scheduled for a meeting in Laredo, Texas, my mind immediately went to the country song, "The Streets of Laredo" sung by Marty Robbins. I wondered if it would resemble the feelings that cowboy ballad brought to my mind so many times. It's interesting when a city has such an "anthem" that connects it with so many people who may never visit in person. As I have traveled throughout the world, so many people will reference "County Roads" when I mention that I am from West Virginia.

The flight to Laredo, Texas was just under an hour from Dallas. We arrived at the small, but very nice airport without a problem. There is a life size sculpture of two horses and two cowboys in front of the airport that gives you the feeling of being in the Old West. We grabbed a taxi to city hall and arrived in plenty of time for our meeting with Assistant City Manager Horacio De Leon, Jr. A large statue of George Washington is in front of City Hall. We learned that each year there is a large festival in his honor. We were greeted by a lovely lady at the City Hall welcome desk, who pointed us to the third floor for our meeting. The Laredo City Hall has tall ceilings and a sweeping staircase in the center of the building. We walked upstairs and met Mr. De Leon, a twenty-year veteran of the city who has held many positions before being named Assistant City Manager.

Mr. De Leon gave us some background information on the city and explained that Laredo is one of the largest inland ports in the United States with over 13,000 trucks entering into the United States each day. The city sits at the southern end of Interstate 35 and on the northern bank of the Rio Grande River. The population in 2010 was 236,191 making it the tenth largest city in Texas. Laredo is a relatively safe city with a low crime rate and a low unemployment rate. The city is largely Hispanic with over 95% of the residents being of Hispanic heritage.

Our meeting concluded and we wanted to sample some local cuisine before heading back to Dallas. We asked the receptionist at city hall for a recommendation. She pointed us just down the street to the Rochas El Catan Grill that has been featured on *The Food Network*. The food was hot, spicy and absolutely delicious. We topped the meal off with a glass of cold lemonade and could not have been more satisfied.

We spent a little time walking through Downtown Laredo and remarked at the colorful displays in the windows. The temperature was in the 90's, which seemed to be tolerated well by the folks on the street but it shortened our walk to about thirty minutes. The summer temperatures are usually in the high 90's and often hits over 100 degrees. We should have gotten a little hint of the climate when we learned that the pro soccer team's name is The Laredo Heat!

I really liked Laredo, enjoying the hospitality and friendliness of the people we met. It has a small town feel and a laid back atmosphere that I love. I'm definitely going to plan another trip to Laredo so that I can enjoy the great food and spend some time walking on "the streets of Laredo".

Los Angeles, California

"I love Los Angeles, and I love Hollywood. They're beautiful.
Everybody's plastic, but I love plastic. I want to be plastic."
Andy Warhol

Los Angeles is such a large and diverse city that it is easy to see many different things and I doubt you could ever truly get your arms around this wonderful city.

Right before I left for my latest trip, Los Angeles suffered a catastrophic water line failure on the UCLA campus. The video of the break was amazing with water spraying hundreds of feet in the air and millions of gallons of water cascading down the steps of campus. The famed Pauley Pavilion, of UCLA Basketball fame was inundated and students were wading through water to get to class. The water line that failed was 93 years old. In talking to some officials with the City of Los Angeles, they pointed out that this was a pretty good lifespan for a pipe that was installed prior to World War I. Thankfully, the City of Los Angeles Public Works Department worked around the clock; the pipe was repaired and traffic restored in just a few days. The local news was showing pictures of the hundreds of cars that were covered in mud and probably a total loss.

As we visited with members of the Los Angeles City Council, Councilmember Tom LaBonge arranged for us to have a private tour of the Los Angeles City Hall. It is an imposing building that reaches over 26 stories. Two young men from Berlin, Germany and Hangzhou, China were our guides. They took us to the observation deck at the top of City Hall and we were able to see for miles in every direction. We could see the iconic HOLLYWOOD sign and Dodger Stadium in the distance. Our guides, Alec and Luke, were recent high school graduates and came to America to serve as interns in Councilman LaBonge's office. I asked them if they had heard the song "Country Roads" and they started singing it. I told them that I was from West Virginia and they seemed very impressed.

It was a treat going to lunch at Philippe's, an old fashioned diner just a block or two from the LA City Hall. It was like turning the clock back fifty years with uniformed ladies behind the lunch counter taking orders and returning your change on little metal trays. It was also "cash only" which is a little shocking in this credit card world. The place was very busy. The bus boys were scurrying around cleaning the modest tables for another group of business people and tourists to take their seats. The food was delicious and looking at the memorabilia on the walls was a history lesson of LA.

Another unique experience was using the Uber car service. If you haven't heard of Uber, it is a car service that is dispatched on the Internet. You simply download the application, type in where you are going and a driver will pick you up. The cost is much lower than a taxi and it is quick and efficient. Our first ride was going into West Hollywood for dinner. A driver named Mike picked us up in his 2014 Nissan Altima. When drivers sign up to be a part of Uber and they have to be screened and have a new mid-sized or larger car. Mike was quite enthusiastic and very engaging. As part of the Uber process, you rate each driver with one to five stars and the driver rates the passenger on the same scale. No money is exchanged with the driver. Your credit card is charged and a receipt emailed to you right after the trip.

We used another driver after dinner, a young teacher who was driving for Uber in the summer for extra money. She had a new Prius and had only been driving for about a week. She was also very positive on Uber and did a great job getting us back to the hotel.

When we were returning to the airport for our flight home, we once again used Uber. Our driver was prompt and got us to the airport on time. It will be interesting to see how this catches on around the country but it is already in many U.S. cities and has also gone worldwide with service in England and France.

So much for another trip to LA, it is such an exciting city. One that offers so much for this vagabond West Virginian!

Marrakech, Morocco

"...writing stories was always a bit like falling in love with a stranger and running off to Marrakech for a long weekend. It didn't have to be successful to be thrilling."
Ann Patchett

When I first heard the song "Marrakech Express" by Crosby, Stills and Nash I could never have dreamed that one day in 2006, I would be walking in the old, walled city and exploring the hundreds of vendors. The occasion was a meeting of the United Cities and Local Governments, an organization that represents cities from throughout the world. I was a little apprehensive since this was in the post 9/11 world and the location was in an area that had terrorist attacks in the past. It was even more eerie when, in 2011, a suicide bomber exploded a bomb in the very square where we had posed for pictures just a few years earlier.

Marrakech is a beautiful city and the sights and sounds overwhelm your senses as you enter into an ancient world seemingly untouched by the passage of time. It is known as the "Red City" or "Ochre City" because of the red sandstone used in construction of many of the buildings. The climate and terrain are similar to the United States Southwest with very hot summers and generally wet winters. Marrakech is on the northern side of the Atlas Mountains and snow can be seen in the distance.

After landing and getting unpacked we decided to take a taxi to the "Old Town". It became an adventure to remember. As we got in a taxi we became aware the driver had apparently jumped the line. His fellow cabbies got in front of our cab while one fellow opened the door and grabbed my wife by the arm. They were letting us know that we needed to get into another taxi, but my wife was thinking we were being kidnapped. The adventure did not end there. Thousands of cars, trucks, horse drawn carts, goats and every type of motorbike you could imagine were converging on the narrow roads and intersections. It is somewhat disconcerting when you see young school children dodging the traffic without so much as a cautious look.

When we entered the square in the old Town, the various vendors looking for a quick tourist buck set upon us. I felt a tug on my shirt and turned around to see a young teenager with two monkeys on a leash. He thrust the monkeys on my shoulder and before I knew it, he was motioning for my wife to take a picture. She snapped a quick picture and the young man had his hand out for a tip. I took out a few coins and handed it to him when he motioned his displeasure. I kept counting out coins and he kept motioning for more. I finally gave him the remainder of my coins and walked away.

There were also cobras dancing to the sound of the flute and one vendor who had a card table set up with hundreds of human teeth. I never did figure out what the teeth were used for.

The food in Morocco was a treat. From a plentiful breakfast to seven course dinners, food is a big part of life in the country. One memorable meal was at an exotic restaurant that featured belly dancing along with fantastic food. Unless you have seen traditional belly dancers, it is hard to appreciate this ancient entertainment. The dancers are very talented and you can see why this art has survived for hundreds of years. The food included a dish called 'Couscous', which is served in a stone dish covered with a woven onion shaped cover.

Marrakech is one of the most interesting places that I've ever visited and I would return if the opportunity presented itself. As Graham Nash famously sang, "Had to get away to see what we could find. Hope the days that lie ahead bring us back to where they've led."

Mexico City, Mexico

"Really, Mexico City has always been this big, complex monster of a city that has always had real problems and needs, and I've always found my way through it in different ways."
Alejandro Gonzalez Inarritu

In November of 2010, I attended the United Cities and Local Governments World Congress in Mexico City, Mexico. UCLG is an international organization headquartered in Barcelona, Spain and represents local governments throughout the world. I have attended several meetings of UCLG in many parts of the world. It is always a great experience to meet with mayors and other officials to share experiences in local government. Mexico City is a very historic city and is home to over 21.2 million citizens, making it the largest city in the western hemisphere and the largest Spanish-speaking city in the world.

Our visit also coincided with the celebration of the 200th Anniversary of Mexican Independence and the 100th Anniversary of the Mexican Revolution. As we walked along the city streets, it was evident that there was something big going on. Bleachers were set up along the streets and the podium was being constructed for the Mexican President, Felipe Calderon, to address millions of people attending the celebration. There was a large police and military presence in the city for the celebration. That was probably fortunate for us as Mexico City is a very dangerous city for citizens and visitors alike. Our hotel advised us to be careful when we ventured into the city and we were also told to avoid any taxicabs other than those connected to the hotel. There are many stories about taxicab drivers kidnapping their passengers and driving to a remote area where they were robbed. Needless to say, we were very cautious and followed our instructions to the letter.

Despite the danger to tourists, the people of Mexico City were very warm and hospitable. We met many people who were very interested in talking to us about the United States and the issues of immigration and other concerns. My travel mates at the conference were Valerie Brown and Lenny Eliason from the National Association of Counties. Valarie was the current President of NACO and Lenny was the President-elect. We enjoyed seeing the sights together and enjoying the fantastic cuisine of Mexico. While I have always been a fan of Mexican food, getting the real thing was a real treat. Mexican cuisine is known for its intense and varied flavors, colorful decoration and a variety of spices.

The architecture of Mexico City is a lot like many of the grand European cities I have visited. The streets are wide and there are few large skyscrapers. Little shops line the streets and many are decorated with a festive décor throughout the year. Like many large cities, there is a lot of graffiti and vandalism in the city center but the neighborhoods adjacent to the downtown are tree lined and generally clean.

Our visit was memorable and the conference showed us a lot of the cultural traditions of Mexico. There were the sounds of dozens of mariachi bands that performed at many of the receptions and events. On the evening of the Presidential address at the National Palace, we were entertained by a unique light show that was projected on the sides of some of the buildings in the Federal District. The lights are controlled by computers and create the illusion of movement on the buildings. It was one of the most unique displays I had ever witnessed. Walking among millions of visitors, we enjoyed the festivities and bid a warm goodbye to the Mexican capital city.

As the plane lifted off from the Benito Juarez International Airport, I looked out the window and got a view of the immense size of Mexico City. The city stretches for miles with the crowded streets and densely populated neighborhoods. I would like to visit Mexico again in the future and maybe see some of the other areas that make up this interesting country. Until next time, *hasta luego* (translation: see you later!).

Minneapolis, Minnesota

"And the sculptor woman was so clever in the way she did it. She had the beret just about to leave my hand. So it's attached to this finger and that's what will keep it there. And I'm looking up at it, so there's no question but that that beret is going to fly".
Mary Tyler Moore

My first introduction to Minneapolis was through *The Mary Tyler Moore Show* when Mary Richards threw her hat in the air in downtown Minneapolis. Having visited the city on a couple of occasions, I see why it is such a popular city. In the winter, it is cold but you can make your way around the city through a web of glass walkways that go from building to building without having to brave the weather. In the summer, it is a beautiful city with flowers and greenery on every corner.

On a recent visit with members of the Minneapolis City Council, I was impressed at the efforts being made to create a sustainable city through several innovative initiatives. Developing a bike friendly environment is evident through the bike share program that is located throughout the city. This gives residents and visitors a way to travel without using cars or other means of transportation. Sitting on the banks of the Mississippi, there are also walking and biking trails that encourage walking and biking.

The city has encouraged and supports a great deal of public art. Large murals are painted on several buildings with one large work being a reproduction of a piece of sheet music that stretches over a city block. Flower pots and sculptures are throughout the city and it has a welcoming appeal. This leads to a good deal of activity on the streets. We walked down one street and it had several dozen food trucks lined up with a wonderful variety of offerings to the many office dwellers spending a pleasant lunch hour outdoors. And, of course, they have a statue of Mary Richards throwing her hat in the air which is a popular tourist spot.

One innovation I saw in the historic Minneapolis City Hall was the use of 'stand up' desks. As we walked into the reception room for City Council, a young lady was typing on a keyboard while standing up. While this looked odd to us, she explained that they have a desk system that elevates to enable the worker to stand at their computer instead of being seated. She said that she alternates between standing and sitting but generally stands more than sits. As we walked back among the dozens of workers in the council offices, we noticed almost all of the workers standing in their cubicles. There are considerable health benefits from standing but this was the first time I had ever seen the concept in practice to this degree.

Minnesota is known for its thousands of lakes. Flying over the city of Minneapolis, it is easy to see the plentiful water supply that resides in a landscape dotted with these varied sizes of lakes. With water issues affecting much of the United States, Minneapolis will have no problem providing adequate water for its residents and businesses.

The food offerings in Minneapolis were varied with some noteworthy local spots. We had lunch at a unique diner called Erbert and Gerbert's and their sandwiches were delicious. Our evening dinner was at an outstanding steakhouse in the heart of the downtown. It was called Manny's and featured a wide array of steaks and seafood. Our waiter was excellent and brought a cart around to show us the size and quality of the steaks before we ordered. Needless to say, we ordered steaks which as good as any I have ever had. My business partner and I shared a dessert and when it arrived, we could have fed half the restaurant with the portion. It was a brownie-like desert with chocolate mousse covered with whipped cream and chocolate syrup. Even the gentlemen at the next table were impressed and started up a conversation with us.

It is easy to see why Minneapolis has remained one of America's most popular cities. The city government seems to be proactive and provide good service to their citizens. The business community works to improve the business climate for the benefit of the residents. While Mary Richards is no longer working the newsroom with Lou Grant and Ted Baxter, Minneapolis is still an Amazing City and one that is worthy of a visit in any season.

Morgantown, West Virginia

Reporter: Is there a New York feel to what's going on in Morgantown?
Coach Huggins: You've never been to Morgantown, have you?
WVU Basketball Coach Bob Huggins

Throughout my life, I have only lived in two cities. One is Clarksburg and the other is Morgantown. In 1968, I packed my popcorn popper and a few other necessities and headed north to enter West Virginia University. It was an exciting time in my life. My five years in Morgantown left an indelible mark on my development as an adult. Morgantown is now a fairly short drive from Clarksburg on Interstate 79 but in 1968, it was a winding road that took nearly an hour to drive. As you entered Morgantown, West Virginia University dominated the landscape and most activities took place at the downtown campus. Mountaineer Field was just down from Woodburn Hall. Game days were eclectic as thousands of fans converged on the stadium as game time approached. Basketball games were held in the old Field House on Beechurst Avenue and held just over 5,000 fans.

During my time in Morgantown, the Personal Rapid Transit System and the Coliseum were under development with major construction going on throughout the city. The Evansdale Campus was growing and the

Towers dormitory complex had two buildings with two more under construction. We took blue and gold buses from Towers to the Downtown campus and rarely were late for a class. Most of the time we would hang out between classes at the Mountainlair rather than riding the bus back to the dorm. High Street was another popular destination with many shops, bars and places to eat. The drinking age at that time was 18 and bars were filled to capacity on most weekends.

After moving back to Clarksburg in 1973, I would often return to Morgantown for games and sometimes to visit the Daniels Men Store on High Street. It was a great experience and as the highway construction made the visit easier. A movie at the Warner Theater and dinner at the Flame restaurant were favorite places to get away to when Clarksburg seemed a little behind the times.

In 2007, I was asked to lead an effort to revitalize the Sunnyside neighborhood in Morgantown. I got reacquainted with many of the places of my younger days. Morgantown has undergone an unbelievable change and is now double the size from when I had previously lived in the city. Evansdale is now as big or bigger than the downtown campus and the PRT celebrated its 40th Anniversary in 2010. Mountaineer Field replaced the downtown stadium and Ruby Hospital is huge compared to the Medical Center of my generation. The traffic in Morgantown has always been an issue but it has really worsened in the past forty years or so. Going from one place to another requires a good deal of planning and finding a parking place is often an adventure.

They say you can never go home again and working in the city made me fondly long for the Morgantown of old. Mutt's Bar, Sunnyside Superette, Mario's Fishbowl and countless other sites do not seem the same. Large apartment complexes dominate the landscape and the university seems to have an insatiable appetite for growth.

I still love Morgantown. I loved working in Sunnyside for five years and getting to meet some of the incredible young people who are making their own memories in the University City. Cities grow and change. Morgantown continues to grow and developers are on every corner with bigger and better ideas. The new Interstate exit in Westover will fundamentally change hundreds of acres of undeveloped property and the new WVU Baseball stadium will draw new fans to the city.

The entire region is impacted by what goes on in Morgantown. Health care, sports, business and culture are all centered within fifty miles of Morgantown. Our airport in Harrison County has received quite a boost by the Big12 teams that fly in and spend money in our area. Housing costs have driven many workers to look at Harrison County as a more affordable market and it has grown our housing supply. My other "hometown" is a part of most West Virginian's lives and I still remember it fondly.

Paris, France

"The first thing that strikes a visitor to Paris is a taxi."
Fred Allen

I have been fortunate to visit the Amazing City of Paris several times in my life. Each visit has been memorable. My first visit was on a trip to the former Soviet Union and we had a layover in Paris. We were to transfer airports, going from Charles De Gaulle to Orly, which are on opposite sides of Paris. When I saw that the layover was five hours, I thought, "What a great time to see the sights of Paris!" I set off with a young man from New York City, as the rest of our group was sitting in the terminal waiting for the bus to take them to the other airport. The group leader asked us what we were going to do if we missed our flight. We laughed and said, "We'll be in Paris!"

We jumped in a cab and told the driver to take us to the Eiffel Tower, as it was the one thing we most wanted to see. It was everything we hoped for and we stood at the base and marveled at the unbelievable structure. We had coffee and a croissant at a cafe and started to think about getting to the airport. As luck would have it, right next to the cafe was an office for Air France. We went in and asked for the best way to get to the airport. The pretty clerk said that a shuttle was just getting ready to leave and we could get on for free. As we pulled up to the terminal, we could see our group sitting on their luggage after a boring bus ride on the outer ring of Paris regretting that they didn't join us on our adventure.

My next trip to Paris was with Pastor David Kates. We attended a conference in Switzerland. I thought it would be nice to see if we could make a short visit to Paris. We boarded the "bullet train" in Geneva and whisked along the countryside at 160 mph.

Pastor Kates was thrilled to get to see Paris for the first time. He took a picture in front of the Eiffel Tower with a little boy who was there with his parents. We visited with a friend of mine who was working for IBM and had an apartment just a short walk from the Seine River. I had met her on a Habitat trip I took to Poland a few years earlier. She hosted us for a delicious lunch in her neighborhood. Pastor Kates and I made a quick visit to the Louvre before boarding the train back to Geneva.

My last trip to Paris was with my wife, Pam. We had the time of our lives. It is the perfect city to be in with someone you love. It feels like you are in a movie as you take a river tour on the Seine and admire the sights and sounds of the city. Paris is a walkable city making it is so enjoyable to stroll down streets and take in the artists and street performers. The food is fantastic and seeing the Eiffel Tower at night is one of the most beautiful sights in the entire world.

Few cities have the allure of Paris and I cannot think of a place that inspires such good feelings as the "City of Light".

Philadelphia, Pennsylvania
City of Brotherly Love

"I love the dignity in the name Philadelphia, but at heart, we're Philly."
Lisa Scottoline

Few cities in the United States can lay claim to the history that has taken place in Philadelphia. From its favorite son, Benjamin Franklin, to the 67 National Historic Landmarks, Philadelphia attracts millions of visitors and brings in over $10 billion in tourism dollars. With a population exceeding 1.5 million citizens, Philadelphia is the fifth largest city in the United States and the largest city in Pennsylvania. William Penn founded the city in 1682 to serve as the capital of the Pennsylvania colony. Philadelphia played an instrumental role in the American Revolution and served as a meeting place for the Founding Fathers who signed the Declaration of Independence in 1776.

While I have visited Philadelphia on several occasions in the past, my most recent trip was one of the most interesting. I stayed at the Union League which is a private club founded in 1862 as a Patriotic Society to support the Union and the policies of President Abraham Lincoln. The building is just a few blocks from City Hall and is a classic Second Empire-style structure with a brick and brownstone façade and two circular stairways that lead to the main entrance on Broad Street. The interior has undergone an extensive renovation and is one of the most luxurious places I have ever visited. They have a very strict dress code. Gentlemen are required to wear a jacket in all of the public areas of the club and in all the restaurants. They even have a cigar bar with a state of the art air filtration system that reduces the smoke associated with old style smoking rooms of the past.

Philadelphia has more sculptures and murals than any other city in the United States. Prominent among them is the large 'clothes pin' that is located across the street from City Hall. Dedicated in 1976, it is 45-foot-tall and is constructed of weathering steel, which gives it a warm, reddish-brown color. During my visit, there was an art exhibition in front of City Hall called 'Red Bull Art of the Can'. It is a national competition to highlight artists who have constructed pieces of art out of the aluminum cans of the Red Bull Energy drink. It was very interesting and the creativity was evident as hundreds of people were standing in line to view the sculptures.

Philadelphia is often described as a 'gritty' city and it is a little rough around the edges. For many years, the population was declining due to the many manufacturing companies abandoning the city in favor of the warmer climates of the South. Recently, however, the city is rebounding and many of the old neighborhoods and industrial areas are attracting younger people. They have revitalized many of the buildings and added a new energy into the city.

As you walked along the streets in the downtown, there were still large banners attached to the light poles to celebrate the visit of Pope Francis which had happened in late September. In speaking with city officials, they were extremely pleased at the papal visit and estimated that over half a million people were in the city for the visit.

Philadelphia certainly qualifies as an Amazing City and is a great place to visit. The trip from Clarksburg is a pleasant five-hour drive through some of the most beautiful scenery in the country. I enjoyed the fall weather and seeing the trees beginning to change color. I look forward to my next visit to the city of brotherly love and having another great Philly Cheesesteak.

Pittsburgh, Pennsylvania

"Just growing up in Pittsburgh and knowing different neighborhoods, having family there and just loving it, it's like no other place."
Wiz Khalifa

I'm probably like a lot of West Virginians when it comes to Pittsburgh. It is a place that we sometimes take for granted. We attend concerts, eat at restaurants, do Christmas shopping and follow the Pirates and Steelers without recognizing what a treasure it truly is. Pittsburgh has stood the test of time and transformed itself from the steel capital of the world to a high tech city of the future. While there are still some rough edges to improve upon, Pittsburgh has created a vibrant appeal and one that serves a much larger area than the 1.2 million residents of Allegheny County, Pennsylvania.

In a recent meeting with Dan Gilman, a new City Councilman from Pittsburgh, we talked about Pittsburgh and its future. Dan is an interesting guy and someone who is part of a youth invasion into politics in the Pittsburgh area. Dan worked for eight years as Chief of Staff for Councilman Bill Peduto. When Bill was elected Mayor of Pittsburgh, Dan was elected to City Council. To say that Dan is enthusiastic about the new Mayor and the future of Pittsburgh is an understatement. I met Mayor Peduto at a recent National League of Cities conference in Seattle. He understands the challenges and seems ready to make some positive changes in the city. In order to make this happen, a lot of people will need to recognize the integral role that the city plays in the life of the entire region.

A recent project called the Power of 32 has spent time analyzing the impact of the thirty-two counties surrounding Pittsburgh and how they can work together to accomplish goals to develop this region into a strong force throughout the country. Serving on the planning committee for the Power of 32, I learned of other regions in both the United States and throughout the world who have transformed from heavy manufacturing into strong, high technology centers that drive the regional economy. The Power of 32 has been funded by a variety of foundations (including the Benedum Foundation who is active in West Virginia) and local businesses that recognize the value of working together.

While the future of Pittsburgh is moving forward, we should remember the valuable history of Pittsburgh and how it fits into many West Virginian's memories. The view coming out of the Fort Pitt tunnels, the Incline, Point State Park with the fountain, the beautiful skyline, Kennywood Park and dozens of other iconic sites that were part of many of our first visits to the "big city". I can remember going to Pirate games as an altar boy at Holy Rosary Catholic Church in Clarksburg, where we made an annual pilgrimage to Forbes Field.

So the next time you take that drive up I-79, think about how your life would be different without the "Steel City".

Rome, Italy

"Rome was a poem pressed into service as a city."
Anatole Broyard

My first visit to Rome could best be described as an accidental trip. I was on a trip to Kiev, USSR on December 31st and as the plane was going from New York to Kiev, via Rome, the group leader discovered that I did not have a visa to enter into the Soviet Union. He assured me that everything would be taken care of when we arrived in Rome, however I knew that this would be difficult since I had entered the Soviet Union on several occasions and obtaining a visa usually takes several weeks in the best of times.

Upon arrival in Rome, the group leader franticly called the Soviet Embassy without success. As the flight to Moscow was being boarded, he looked at me and said that they would have to leave me since the embassy was closed for New Years. He gave me a piece of paper with an Italian travel agency's number and said to call them after New Year's Day. I watched the group wave at me as they boarded the plane for Moscow. So began my adventure in Rome, by myself, with no luggage and a slip of paper.

As I walked out of the Rome airport, I saw a sign that said, "Holiday Inn-St. Peters". I figured that at least they would speak English and be able to direct me to the Soviet Embassy to obtain the visa, if at all possible.

I settled into the room and turned on the television to CNN, the only channel in English. I went to bed after a long day and didn't give a thought to it being New Year's Day the next morning. I slept soundly and was awakened about 9:30 a.m. by the sound of the television that had played all night. CNN was reporting on the New Year's celebrations throughout the world. They flashed on the Pope giving his New Year's blessing at St. Peter's Square in Vatican City. I made a mental note that I would like to see that sometime in my life.

After showering, I thought I would explore Rome since the Soviet Embassy was not open on New Year's Day. The cab dropped me off at the Vatican and as I walked into the square, I was surprised at how dirty it was. There were paper cups and trash blowing throughout the area. It was only then that I realized that only a few hours before, there had been hundreds of thousands of people listening to the Pope give his message. I felt kind of stupid, not realizing that I could have seen this incredible event if only I had put two and two together and gotten up a little earlier.

Walking around the Vatican, I felt like I had been taken back in time. It is such a gorgeous place and the buildings are so old and beautiful that you feel like you are living in another time. The pillars surrounding St. Peter's Square are huge. You wonder how they were constructed so many years ago. It was also interesting to see the hundreds of nuns and priests walking around and riding bikes. Quite a sight!

I still needed to obtain my visa and attempt to catch up to my group in the Soviet Union but I planned to make the best of this accidental visit to this Amazing City.

Taking a cab the next day, I headed to the Soviet Embassy. It was located in an old house with a long brick walk. As I entered the house, I opened the first door I saw. A large man in a suit looked at me with a scowl and shouted something in Russian that I took as "Close the door!" I finally found an office with a secretary and explained that I needed to obtain a visa to enter the Soviet Union. She also did not appear to understand English. A young woman came up to me and asked if I needed some help. She was Swedish and worked for a travel agency in Rome. She offered to assist me but said she was not sure that it was possible to get a visa in such a short time. I watched as she explained my plight to the secretary and saw her shake her head "no" on several occasions. Finally, she pulled an official looking piece of paper from her desk and started to type. She took a large seal from her desk and put it on the document. The last step was for the Soviet Ambassador to sign the visa. She led me into a room and I saw the man in the suit that had yelled at me. He was the Ambassador!

With my newly minted visa, I could not get a flight into Moscow for two days, so I decided to see as many sites as I could in this beautiful city. My first stop was the Spanish Steps. The Spanish Steps were constructed in 1723-1725 to connect the Piazza di Spagna to the Piazza Trinita del Monti. The Spanish Steps are a popular tourist spot and hundreds of people sit on the steps to watch visitors from throughout the world walk by. I think the steps were my favorite spot in Rome. The Spanish Steps are just a short distance from the beautiful *Trevi Fountain*, one of the most recognized fountains in the world. The fountain is over 86 feet high and 161 feet wide. The intricate sculptures are beautiful. I did what millions of tourists throughout history have done, I threw a coin in the fountain, insuring a return visit in my lifetime.

As you walk around Rome, it is amazing to realize that most of the landmarks are fairly close together. As I walked down one street, something caught my eye. It was the Colosseum. In its day, the Colosseum held between 50,000 and 80,000 spectators who watched Gladiators battle fierce lions. Although it is partially ruined because of damage by devastating earthquakes and stone robbers, it is one of Rome's most popular tourist destinations.

As I left the Rome airport on my journey to the Soviet Union, I knew that I would never forget my "accidental" trip to one of the most beautiful cities in the world. I have told many people that if they could only visit one city, Rome would be the one I would recommend.

San Antonio, Texas

"My grandmother didn't live to see us begin our lives in public service. But she probably would have thought it extraordinary that just two generations after she arrived in San Antonio, one grandson would be the mayor and the other would be on his way - the good people of San Antonio willing- to the United States Congress."
Julian Castro

O ne of America's true Amazing Cities is San Antonio, Texas. With the Riverwalk, the Alamo and a host of other attractions, San Antonio is growing and developing a reputation as a great city to live in or visit. I've had the opportunity to visit the city on several occasions and I am always impressed with the unique architecture and friendly people. The hundreds of restaurants give you a wide variety of food choices but you cannot go wrong with the Mexican cuisine. San Antonio is a city that seems to spread out forever with streets that are home to thousands of single story houses and commercial buildings.

Over the years I have met several of San Antonio's city officials and have always been impressed with their dedication to making the city a better place to live. Henry Cisneros was Mayor of San Antonio and became President of the National League of Cities in 1986. He was a true superstar of local government and did many great things to build San Antonio into the city it is today. Mayor Cisneros went on to become Secretary of Housing and Urban Development (HUD) and remains a force in the housing industry with his City View Housing Development Organization. Mayor Julian Castro also became Secretary of Housing and Urban Development in the Obama administration after serving the citizens of San Antonio. I served on the Board of Directors of the National League of Cities with Mayor Castro and you could tell that he was a very talented young man headed for higher office.

I had recently met the current San Antonio Mayor, Ivy Taylor who is the first African-American mayor of the city. She served on city council and was appointed Mayor when Julian Castro went to HUD. She is a graduate of Yale University and has an extensive background in urban planning, which is needed with all the growth and development in the city.

The city council in San Antonio is one of the youngest in all of the major cities in America. They are required to run every two years and can only serve a maximum of eight years. This leads to a good bit of turnover in the city government and seems to always attract a talented group of young people willing to devote their time to public service. I have been most impressed to see the way they have embraced technology and innovation to move the city forward.

I would probably be remiss if I did not mention the climate of this very southern city. It is hot in the summer and very humid at times. On a recent visit in August, it was around 98 degrees and the locals were remarking that it was normally a little bit hotter at that time of year. You can see the logic behind the "siesta", as it seems impossible to work in that oppressive heat. The residents seemed to tolerate the heat pretty well but it was pretty tough on this West Virginian!

The public art and open spaces in the city are very well done. They give the feel of a festive occasion as you walk throughout the city. Fountains and splash parks are prevalent and the Spanish tile work is present on many bridges and other areas. While the city is dealing with the effects of a prolonged drought, they keep the landscape in good condition with plantings that are tolerant of the lack of water. The Alamo is undergoing a redevelopment and adding to the natural draw of this national landmark.

San Antonio holds a warm spot in my heart as the people are probably its biggest asset. When we visited Councilmember Shirley Gonzales' office in her ward, several of the ladies working in the office introduced themselves and went out of their way to make us feel welcome. I hope to visit San Antonio many more times in my life and look forward to seeing great things on the horizon for this Amazing City.

San Diego, California

"I was homeless and I was in San Diego and I started singing in a local coffee shop and people started coming to hear me sing."
Jewel

When you hear about the wonderful Southern California climate and lifestyle, no city does it better than San Diego. The downtown area is filled with jogging trails, benches and interesting sights and sounds. The light rail service and the bicycle program make it easy to get around the city and seems to reduce the traffic congestion of many cities in California. The San Diego Convention Center is one of the larger ones in the United States and features a growing assortment of hotels within a short walk of most of the downtown. An interesting feature that I found in the city was a noticeable absence of traffic signals. A lot of the intersections have stop signs and this seems to work very well. The traffic flow moved along without long waits. Pedestrian movement also seemed to move pretty well. This might be a sign of things to come in more cities.

San Diego is also moving forward into the Smart City concept with an increasing amount of technology and innovation being incorporated into many of the city functions. I had the opportunity to speak with city officials in the environmental services department about the upgrade to many of the streetlights in the city. Street lighting is no longer just a "bulb on a pole" but rather an integrated communication tool that can give city leaders a growing array of data. Parking control, public safety, Homeland Security, city planners and others can use the poles to improve city services and security for the citizens and visitors. Public Wi-Fi can also be used to enable smart apps to guide visitors through the city and coordinate with businesses to offer specials and other incentives.

One of the things that San Diego does and is being copied by an increasing number of cities is to employ a director of public partnerships. As cities look for ways to offset declining tax revenue and create public-private partnerships, having a dedicated office to facilitate these opportunities is an idea that seems to fit well in city governments. Sponsorship of events or assisting public activities are natural ways of joining the city with corporate entities. The San Diego model insures that companies involved in these partnerships are ethical and above board and the city has final say in the partnership agreements.

As with any growing city, San Diego has some growing pains that will need to be addressed as more and more people are moving to the city. Housing affordability is a challenge and was mentioned by many people when I asked them what they thought could be improved in the city. Workforce housing is tough to find and people have to travel an increasing distance to find an affordable place to live. Another thing mentioned by our Uber driver was the possible relocation of the airport. San Diego International Airport is located just a few minutes from downtown and is convenient and easy to get to. The problem is that it is landlocked and if a new airport is built, it will be a considerable distance from the city. A new football stadium is also in discussion. This has many of the citizens worried that the San Diego Chargers will relocate if they are not able to keep up in the "Stadium Wars" happening across the country. These will be delicate issues moving forward for the city government and will impact the future livability of the city.

Hopefully, San Diego will keep moving forward and become an even more Amazing City. It is hard to beat the climate and accessibility of this beautiful city.

Selma, Alabama

"Change does not roll in on the wheels of inevitability,
but comes through continuous struggle. And so we must
straighten our backs and work for our freedom. A man can't
ride you unless your back is bent."
Martin Luther King, Jr.

Several years ago, I was asked to represent the
National League of Cities at a housing rehabilitation project in Selma, Alabama. Selma is located along
the Alabama River in the heart of the Black Belt. I was
not sure what to expect. I had studied the Civil Rights
movement and the image of Sheriff Bull Conner's men
beating the marchers on the famous Selma to Montgomery march at the Edmund Pettis Bridge left an indelible
mark on my memory.

I flew into Montgomery and rented a car for the fifty-four mile drive to Selma. As I got closer, I could see the
Edmund Pettis Bridge in the distance. It is an imposing
structure and one that most of us have seen hundreds
of times as the footage from the sixties is regularly
replayed on news stories and documentaries of that era.
I drove slowly over the bridge and took my first look at
the city of Selma. Selma is about the size of Clarksburg
and has a downtown that is somewhat similar with an
aging downtown and many historic buildings.

I stayed at a hotel within sight of the bridge. The St.
James Hotel is an old hotel and is listed on the National
Register of Historic Places. It takes you back in history
with ceiling fans in the lobby and rooms that feature

high ceilings and heavy drapes. The hotel had fallen into disrepair like much of the downtown until the city put together a plan to restore and operate the hotel. They did a great job of restoration and the hotel is leading the effort to revitalize the downtown.

After several trips to Selma, I fell in love with the people and the city. While there are significant racial issues present in the city, the people work very hard to overcome their very violent past. Poverty is a persistent problem in the city but the citizens are committed to building a new city with a new future.

Selma is a city that every American, both black and white, should visit in their lifetime. You will never forget the feeling of standing on the Edmund Pettis Bridge and remembering the sacrifices made to insure every American the right to vote and participate in our great democracy. Truly an Amazing City!

Soweto, South Africa

"If there are dreams about a beautiful South Africa, there are also roads that lead to their goal. Two of these roads could be named Goodness and Forgiveness."
Nelson Mandela

As we boarded the small bus to visit Soweto, I was not prepared for the experience in visiting this desperately poor area of over 1.3 million residents. Soweto stands for South Western Townships and was once a separate city before becoming part of Johannesburg. We passed hospitals and clinics with AIDS prevention murals painted on the concrete walls. The streets were littered with papers and very little green grass was evident. The housing was a combination of concrete block structures and street after street of shacks, built of tin and wood. Surrounding the city were huge mountains of slag from the extensive mining activity. We learned that these mountains of crushed stone contain mercury that was used in the mining process and often blows into Soweto in huge dust storms. The population is predominantly black and the most common language is Zulu.

Soweto was the home to Nelson Mandela. His red brick house is a major tourist center in the Orlando section of Soweto. Bullet marks in the bricks are evidence of the bitterness displayed towards Mandela and the efforts of the apartheid government to try to destroy the freedom movement. Bishop Desmond Tutu's home is nearby. The memory of both men is prominent in the residents of Soweto. There are also memorials to the struggle to end apartheid with the most prominent being the memorial and museum celebrating the life of Hector Pieterson, the first student killed during the 1976 uprising in Soweto. As I walked around Soweto, it was remarkable that these events took place during my lifetime and many of the prominent people are still living.

We took some time to visit the Kliptown Youth Center, which is located in one of the oldest and poorest sections of Soweto. The program was founded in 2007 and works with the youth to improve their lives. I was so inspired by these young people. They live in shacks and disease is rampant yet they work together to help those less fortunate. The center is a group of buildings in the center of a collection of shanty type housing. There are no utilities or infrastructure. Portable toilets are located along the street and are the only facilities available. Electricity is available only from a single wire that has been spliced into the overhead wires along the road. Yet the Kliptown Youth Center performs dance programs and sells T-shirts to raise money. The leader of the group, himself only in his early twenties, explained that the youth do not want charity but to raise money on their own efforts. Our group bought several T-shirts and enjoyed the traditional African dancing.

One of the most prominent sights in Soweto is the Orlando Towers, two large cooling towers of the former Orlando Power Station. The towers can be seen for miles and feature the largest mural in all of South Africa. There is a suspension bridge between the towers and many people bungee jump and BASE jump from a platform in the middle of the bridge. They also have a huge swing that lets people swing into the cooling tower, an experience that sounded more dangerous than I was willing to attempt.

Soweto is one of the most inspiring places I have ever visited. Amongst overwhelming poverty, people are working to make things better. The children are learning computer skills and teaching each other to read. When I remarked about how difficult things are for these children, they explained that as soon as someone moves out of these tin shacks, another family moves in because conditions are so bad in other parts of the country. It is worth noting that some nicer housing is springing up in parts of Soweto as people get work and seek to improve their housing.

There was also evidence of the Bill and Melinda Gates Foundation having an impact on the AIDS crisis. Many of the leaders we met told of friends and family who have been treated through the generosity of the Foundation.

Tucson, Arizona

Solar power is the last energy resource that isn't owned yet
- nobody taxes the sun yet.
Bonnie Raitt

Visiting Tucson, Arizona has always been a special occasion for me. I always seem to find additional reasons to return to this beautiful city. The appeal of the great weather and the Southwest architecture gives a visitor a lot to like and many things to see. Most people think of Arizona as a flat, desert terrain with little change in elevation. Flying into Tucson quickly dispels that impression with the beautiful mountains surrounding the city. The weather is also reasonably pleasant with the evenings cooling off quite a bit.

On this visit to Tucson, I once again visited the City Council office of Ward 4, which has been held for over 20 years by my good friend, Councilwoman Shirley Scott. I've known Shirley for several years through the National League of Cities conferences. She is one of the most respected city officials in the state of Arizona. Her ward is one of the largest in the United States and encompasses over 100 square miles. People who are not familiar with city governments might not realize the difficulties of governing such a large area and how disconnected the citizens feel when they are so far from the center of town and the city hall.

Councilwoman Scott saw the need for a field office to serve her ward and decided that they were going to develop a "green" building to compliment her passion for energy efficiency and sustainability.

The Ward 4 office was built in 1999 and is one of the pioneering buildings in the solar energy and sustainability movement. The building sits in the middle of a beautiful park area and is a center of activity much of the year. In talking with Councilwoman Scott's Chief of Staff, I learned that the building has outlived some of the solar innovations. New technology has been developed that is even more energy efficient and technologically advanced. This is exciting and goes to prove that those who led the effort for sustainability were on the right track.

Another fascinating thing to see in Tucson is the massive parking lots for decommissioned aircraft. As you leave the airport, you pass the Pima Air Museum which has an impressive array of aircraft; but, that is only the beginning of the journey. A short drive and you suddenly see rows and rows of U.S. Air Force planes that have been parked in neat rows. Thousands of planes of all sizes are parked. Most have the windows and engines covered with what looks to be tape and heavy tarpaulins. I learned that the climate in Tucson is perfect for the storage of these aircraft because they can exist in this area for many years without significant deterioration.

Tucson is a growing city with much new housing being constructed. The mostly one story houses are attractive and give you the feel of the Southwest with cactus in the yards and adobe on much of the exterior. Energy and water conservation are important parts of the growth of the city. Tucson is a leader in this movement. Solar farms are plentiful and much of the terrain is respectful of the need for water for drinking and other uses. The occasional golf course is unusually green but even they have instituted water conservation measures.

I look forward to visiting Tucson again and might even take in a University of Arizona football game coached by former West Virginia University coach, Rich Rodriguez. So long from the Amazing City of Tucson, Arizona.

Wroclaw, Poland

"As we build houses we also build community — not just
a neighborhood but a genuine sense of community that
stretches from cities to towns around the globe. The community we seek to build in partnership with God is his
beloved community. It is Kingdom building, and the Bible
— that great adventure story of God's partnership with his
creation — is our building manual."
Clive Rainey

After a couple of days in Krakow, we boarded a bus
for the three-hour trip to our Habitat building site
in Wroclaw. The countryside was beautiful, with fields
of sunflowers going on for miles. Wroclaw is in Western
Poland and was part of Germany until after World War
II when it was made part of Poland under the terms of
the Potsdam Conference. It was previously called Bre-
slau when it was part of Germany. During various times
in history it has been part of Poland, Germany, Bohe-
mia, Hungary, the Austrian Empire and Prussia. It has
a population of 632,067 making it the fourth largest city
in Poland.

While I have been involved with Habitat for Humanity for many years and participated in many builds, both
locally and in various cities in the United States, the
trip to Poland was a new adventure for me. There were
about seventeen of us on the work team. We stayed at a
modest motel about ten miles away from the work site.
The participants on the work team were from throughout the United States and Canada. We quickly became

friends and shared stories of our hometowns. I was the only one from West Virginia and it was interesting getting to know people of various ages and backgrounds.

The worksite was in a rural area and we would have breakfast at the motel and board a small bus to head to work each day. Unlike the builds in the United States, the Polish Habitat group was building a large group of duplexes. We were tasked with constructing the foundations for three of the buildings. It was pretty tough work as there were not a lot of modern tools or machines. We spent several days assembling heavy metal forms in which to pour the concrete for the foundations. It was grueling work and on mornings when it rained, we would be in mud up to our ankles. There was a Polish foreman and a helper to instruct us exactly where we were to place the forms.

After a week of hammering on the ancient forms, we were awaiting the arrival of the large concrete trucks to pour the foundations. It was a big disappointment when a large truck showed up delivering bags of cement and a dump truck of sand. The next week was filled with lifting heavy bags of cement and shoveling sand into mixers. Some on the team would operate the mixers and others would line up with wheelbarrows to shuttle the wet mix into the forms. It was some of the hardest work I had ever done and at the end of the day, we were ready for some rest and relaxation.

Evenings were filled with a Polish feast at the motel followed by a couple of hours at the local pub drinking the local brew. It was amazing how close you become to the team members as you work beside them each day. We would laugh and tell stories like we knew each other from grade school.

We would also interact with the local population who would come up to us to see the "Americans" who had come to build houses in their country. The people were very friendly. Many knew English and some had visited the United States. We came to appreciate their work ethic and how they endured some pretty tough times and still had smiles on their faces. We got to meet some of the families that were going to live in the homes we were building. It was touching to see young children standing in the mud where their bedrooms would soon be. The families participated in the building when their schedules permitted. It was nice getting to know them.

The Habitat Global Village Program changes lives and gives families a future. But, it also has a profound impact on the lives of the volunteers who travel across oceans to toil and learn.

The lesson learned in Creating Amazing Cities is that it is critical to engage in our communities. It is difficult to truly understand our cities until you have stood side by side with citizens working to improve their neighborhoods.

Closing Thoughts

This book has been in my head for most of my adult life. I thought would be a difficult task finding enough material to describe my thoughts. Instead, it has been a more daunting task to edit the book down into the pages that you have just read.

I hope you have enjoyed the stories and the ideas that can make your city, an Amazing City. My intent has never been to prescribe a "cookie cutter" approach to local government. How boring would that be? Rather, I believe that if you take the things that you have been blessed with and maximize them to the fullest, you will achieve your goals.

A city should breathe, a city should celebrate and, on occasion, a city should cry. Amazing Cities are built on the shoulders of those who came before. They are not the province of any individual but rather a collective mixture of diversity and hope.

I know that some may feel this is a little too simple; that an Amazing City needs dozens of towering cranes and miles of chain link fence. Does a young child care if you have the largest skyscraper in the world if she goes to bed hungry?

My wish is that you see the potential in your city and do something to make it Amazing. Do not be put off by the critics for they will not last. Be inspired by the dreamers, but celebrate the workers for they will build an Amazing City that those who enter will enjoy for years to come.

When in doubt, Be Amazing!